Elsie Hack
Follow Through

TEACHING through Sensory-Motor Experiences

Edited by John I. Arena

Assisted by Bonnie Harrington
and the editorial staff
of Academic Therapy

ACADEMIC THERAPY PUBLICATIONS
1539 Fourth Street
San Rafael, California 94901

©

Copyright 1969

DeWitt Reading Clinic, Inc.

All rights reserved. This book, or parts thereof, may not be reproduced in any form without permission from the publisher.

Printed in the United States of America.

INTRODUCTION

WE KNOW today that many children who were formerly called lazy, stubborn, or indifferent are children whose learning and behavior patterns are inconsistent and inefficient. Although they are intellectually adequate or above average in many cases, these youngsters are continual frustrations to their parents, their teachers, their friends — and to themselves. In spite of the dedicated efforts of many, they can correctly be referred to as functional underachievers. They are simply not performing as they should and could with the appropriate direction and assistance.

The bewilderment over the inconsistent performance and varying patterns of response of these youngsters has lead to the evolution of dozens of new phrases — some medical, some regional, some symptomatic, some legal, some educational. Terms such as perceptually impaired, neurologically handicapped, educationally delayed, and many others, are no longer considered to be descriptive of isolated categories. Rather they are now viewed as being many ways of describing the same but diversified problem.

Because those who work with children want to know how they learn, why they fail, and how to help them, a movement has been initiated that is making an impact on all phases of educational programing. This new awareness is sharpening our understanding of the skills of communication.

It has been long accepted that competence in reading, writing, spelling, and numbers is basic to higher academic performance. It is just becoming recognized that the communication skills are themselves resting on another series of more basic skills, which must first develop and become integrated. When these basic skills — for any of a variety of reasons — are deficient or not sufficiently internalized, academic problems will inevitably result.

In this compilation of new articles, the authors — all experienced in working with children — focus on those areas that they have found to be poorly developed or inefficiently and inconsistently integrated in functionally underachieving children. We hope, as they do, that the strategies they describe will be fashioned, augmented, and refined by others to suit the specific needs of each unique child in each unique setting.

JOHN I. ARENA
Editor

CONTENTS

Introduction	John I. Arena	iii
Sensory-Motor Sequencing Experiences in Learning	R. G. Heckelman	1
Integrating Form Perception	Floria Coon-Teters	13
Building Patterns of Retention	Harold B. Helms	19
Hand-Eye Coordination	Shirley H. Linn	27
Laterality and Directionality	Sheila Doran Benyon	35
Body Image and Body Awareness	Grace Petitclerc	47
Tactile-Kinesthetic Approaches to Learning	Lena L. Gitter	63
Relating Body Awareness and Effortless Motion to Visual Training	C. V. Lyons Emily Bradley Lyons	77
Visual Perception and Discrimination	Donald W. Hardy Beverly B. Casebeer	87
Tuning In	Martha Serio Jane Faelchle	95
A Map in the Head	Jack Wahl	105
Arithmetic and Language Skills Developed Through Emphasis on Counting Sequences	Florence A. Sharp	111
Outer Space of the Inner Child	Mary Lu Kost	121
About the Authors		135

Sensory-Motor Sequencing Experiences in Learning

R. G. Heckelman

SEQUENCING of sensory-motor skills, or a progressive remedial program of sensory-motor skills, is a necessary part of almost all neurologically based rehabilitation learning programs. In my opinion, this approach does not, in itself, constitute a "program." If undertaken as a total program, it may well obscure the multisensory approach to the correction of learning disorders.

Most learning disorders form a syndrome and originate in a constellation of disorders which differ in each child. A sensory-motor sequencing program is at best only a part of a multisensory approach to the problem. Such a program may be needed only in part by some children and not at all by others. The common practice today of subjecting large numbers of children solely to a sensory-motor training program is wasteful of both the teacher's and the children's time.

Sensory-motor training programs in themselves do not always prevent learning problems, and they bear a close resemblance to the old-time, spring remedy of sulphyr and molasses — an untasty concoction which was forced down the throats of children in hopes that its powerful ingredients might purge the system and prevent disease in the body.

Sensory-motor sequencing experiences should be used for the restoration of learning functions. These experiences should use the principle of reorganization of neural pathways which are not adequately functioning for carrying out the learning task properly. A. R. Luria states: " . . . functional systems are characterized by a certain degree of mobility and that one task may be performed by several different methods based on different combinations of active brain units."[1] Frederick C. Thorne says: " . . . the organism strives to maintain the highest possible level of integration at all times."[2] He refers to fifteen postulates found in clinical experience. We will use only his first five and the thirteenth postulates, as they are more nearly related to sensory-motor integration.

1. Behavior may be integrated on many levels of structure and/or function, ranging from the lower-level psychophysiological functions to the highest-level psychosocial interactions.

---

[1] A. R. Luria, *Human Brain and Psychological Processes* (New York, N.Y.: Harper and Row, 1966), p. 65.

[2] Frederick C. Thorne, *Integrative Psychology* (Brandon, Vermont: Clinical Psychology, 1967), p. 8.

2. Each level of functioning acts as a necessary substratum for succeeding higher levels.

3. Disorders of lower-level integrations must necessarily disturb higher-level functions dependent upon them.

4. Under certain conditions, disorders of higher-level functions may radiate down to disturb lower-level functions.

5. Intact functioning on lower levels makes possible functionally autonomous and qualitatively different functions on higher levels.

13. All behaviors reflect the integrative status of the whole person, which simultaneously senses, perceives, learns, retains, feels, thinks, and acts as a global unit. The attempt to deal with functions separately is a logical and semantic artifact.

If sensory-motor learning experiences are maintained in their proper relationship to the total treatment of constellations of defects, we can now define areas which would fall within the following sensory-motor treatment categories.

In children, we attempt to remedy the various types of malfunctions through psychophysiological gross- and fine-motor activities. In the literature, these types of activities are generally identified under general headings such as: body image, body-space integration, balance, laterality, tactile discrimination, rhythm, direction, time sense, and reaction.

The teacher who is confronted with these numerous sensory-motor categories should ask whether she should use all approaches with her students, and which process may be more important than the other to the individual student. This question is answered when the constellation-of-defect approach is used, as we now know all of the above defects are not likely to be found in all children with learning disorders. A severe defect in one or two areas does not necessarily mean that all other areas are likewise defective and in need of remediation techniques.

The teacher should choose the most intact areas for the neural rerouting process toward the more severely damaged areas during the sensory training program. We will present some practical sensory-motor activities on a sequential basis following the nine activity areas previously identified.

BODY IMAGE

THE BODY IMAGE, a part of self-awareness, is what a person thinks of his own physical body and his belief as to how it looks to others. It is an important part of the global system of the individual. Many neurologically handicapped children do not have complete awareness of the total organization of their bodies, nor can they manage integration of the body parts. When asked to reproduce an image which is similar to their own, they are apt to draw a distortion of the body and even to omit important body parts. One of the first steps in making sure that the child is able to identify and understand the relationship of his own body parts is for him to point, on command, to parts of his own body. After he is able to identify the various parts of the body, such as the eyes, mouth, feet, knees, elbows, he can be requested to identify parts of the body in pictures. The teacher might like to make a large copy of the child's body by having him lie on the floor on a paper and

SENSORY-MOTOR SEQUENCING

tracing around him, proceeding then to smaller-size body images and eventually to the identification of the major parts of animal bodies, such as horses, dogs, lions, etc. The child might be asked to identify corresponding parts of the animals' bodies and his own.

Following the child's identification of the parts of his own body and the matching of body parts, he may proceed to duplicate body parts through the use of clay modeling or assembling wooden or plastic puzzles which are made up of body parts that are cut into segments. The progression would be from a large-size puzzle, having three, four, five, and six-pieces, to more complicated puzzles which may have as many as twenty-five to thirty parts. These puzzles should not be presented too soon, and they should not be too complicated, as confusion and misdirection must be avoided.

Games employing gymnastics are a more advanced form of identification of body parts. On command, the children are asked to make movements with the left hand and the left leg, then with the right hand and the right leg. Next they proceed to doing cross-over exercises which involve action that crosses the midline of the body in both directions.

This type of body-part identification training is frequently seen as a part of nursery-school curriculums, but the training may have to be repeated again for older children who have neurological involvement, if testing reveals a discrepancy in the child's knowledge of his own body image.

BODY-SPACE INTEGRATION

AFTER a neurologically handicapped child has become thoroughly oriented to his own body image, he must begin to use the body parts in space in an integrated fashion. Failure to manipulate his body successfully in space may deprive the child of experiences in making many visual, tactile, and manipulative contacts, and it may cut off opportunities to learn through alternate neural channels.

Body-space integration involves, as well as the child's ability to move through space and to locate objects in space correctly, the ability to imitate body spatial relationships.

If outdoor equipment is available, the children may be given the opportunities to crawl through hollow metal drums, concrete conduits, mazes, or in and around constructed pathways which also involve stooping, twisting, and going around corners. A series of boxes may be set in patterns to form a pathway that is narrow and that has sharp turns or corners so that the child must squeeze through and make turns both to the left and the right. This series may be duplicated in the classroom if sufficient space is available. Ropes may be suspended between low poles so that a child will have to climb over or under ropes of various heights in order to develop a sensitivity to space requirements and limitations. The same procedure is followed as with other motor training acts wherein large-muscle movements are required first. Children may be started with simply walking or running between objects and then graduated to more difficult obstacles requiring crawling and the twisting of the body.

The second phase of body-space integration training is when the child imitates

SENSORY-MOTOR

other people who are using their bodies in varied positions in space. The models standing directly in front of the child, lifts one leg, raises one leg to the side, stands with one foot on a box, or extends the arms sideways, above the head, or at a forty-five-degree angle. Perhaps it is best to start with the lower extremities in setting up these varied exercises so that the child is able to look at the model and also at his own legs to see if he is duplicating the positions of the model.

The last phase would be duplication of both arm and hand positions, and from this, moving to combined hand-and-leg spatial combinations.

If video tape is available, children should be photographed as they go through these patterns. When the video tape is played back, the child can see his actual body positions from a positive perspective rather than seeing himself reflected in a mirror. Samples of video tape showing various responses of the child may be stored, then played back later to show his improvement.

BALANCE SEQUENCE

THE BALANCE SEQUENCE combines elements of body-space integration, laterality, rhythm, and direction. Balance plays a large role in the development of laterality. Balancing seems to focus the child's conscious thinking more sharply on his body since he has to make an effort to maintain himself in a state of equilibrium.

Children should be started at the sequence level at which they are able to succeed. If children are able to achieve the first steps of a sequence easily on the first attempt, they should be passed on to the next highest sequence immediately.

The balance sequencing seems to fall into two categories. The first is done on the ground level and demands a lesser degree of need for equilibrium but still helps in the establishment of laterality and directionality. At the second level, the equilibrium of the child is put under more stress, and he needs to concentrate more to maintain his balance. At ground level, some of the sample exercises are as follows:

Ground level.

• The child observes and copies a normal walk, arms swinging naturally at his sides in opposition to leg movement. If the child is unable to perform this action, mold the correct action by having someone assist the child to form the correct pattern.

• The child walks back and forth between two mirrors, observing his own walking pattern.

Note: It is recommended, if possible, that video tape be used in place of the mirrors so the child is able to observe, without involvement, his own walking, rhythm, and patterning.

• Pathways are laid out with tape, chalk, rope, or paint. The child is encouraged to walk within the path limits. The pathways are made increasingly narrower and more complicated as practice progresses.

A preliminary approach to the second level begins when the child raises his body slightly off the ground. Jumping games and patterned steps with alternating leaping, hopping, and jumping activities are in this category. There is a wide variety of jumping exercises which help develop the child's sense of balance.

Raised level.

• The child walks up and down three or four stair steps, using one step at a time — right foot first, then left — bringing the second foot up to the same level as the first. Next he jumps up and down the steps with both feet together. He then progresses to a normal, alternate-foot ascending and descending of the stairs.

Walking boards are widely used in vision training programs by some optometrists, and they are also used in many schools. These are two-by-four inch boards, about twelve feet long, which simulate the old fence-rail walking that children did years ago. The children walk the boards by extending the left foot forward and bringing the right foot up, then moving the right foot forward and bringing the left foot up. They then progress to walking with the left and right feet alternating across the boards. They may move across them sideways and backwards after they have conquered the preceding sequences.

Balance boards allow the child to rotate at any angle and are helpful in establishing balance. The bottom of the balance board is rounded. The child stands on the square platform above the rounded portion and rolls from side to side, trying to balance himself by the distribution of his own weight. A systematic approach to the balance-beam walking board and other balance exercises, as well as rope-jumping sequencing, is found in the book, *Play with a Purpose*.[3] There are many other activities in this book that can be adapted for children with educational handicaps, such as games with balls, and it is helpful that they are sequentially organized and graded according to the difficulty of the activity.

LATERALITY

LATERALITY, or development of right and left determination, seems to precede direction development. Most children have already determined body-side use preference before beginning school and have established reference points for the right and left sides of their body. In the well-integrated, normal child, right and left presents no problem or organization and relationship. Each side of the body functions differently in space and has its own individual meaning. The educationally handicapped child may have to learn to coordinate the left- and right-side nervous systems, since they are by nature semi-independent systems, in order to develop the correct motor directions so essential to the reading task.

All operations and training of laterality in a child should be continued only if the actions are performed instantaneously; hesitation denotes conflicting impulses coming through the nervous system.

It is recommended that the training again start, through large-muscle group. using body, legs, and arms. One of the first ways of developing total body laterality would be to have the child lie on his back, and on command, roll to the left

---

[3] Marion H. Anderson, Margaret E. Elliott, and Jean La Berge, *Play with a Purpose: Elementary School Physical Education* (New York, N.Y.: Harper and Row, 1966), pp. 90-91.

and then back on his back. On further command, he would roll to his right. Following this, he could be requested to put his left leg over his right leg and back, then his left arm over the right side of his body and back.

N. C. Kephart describes a device that is helpful in establishing laterality.[4] Patterns are laid out on the floor with two distinct designs. The first one indicates where the left foot is to be placed; the second one, a contrasting pattern, shows where the right foot should be placed. After walking through these patterns many times, the patterns are shifted about so that the child leads with alternate feet. The patterns become more complicated as the child demonstrates he is able to handle the task.

Another primary activity which helps in developing laterality is to paint a line or stretch a rope across the floor along which the child is asked to move sideways. He walks down the length of the line or rope without touching it with his toes — going first to his left and then repeating the action to the right. He may repeat this maneuver with his back to the rope, looking at the rope over his shoulder, and again going both in a left and right direction. A more complicated movement would be to have him step across the rope with the left foot, bringing up the right foot from the other side of the rope, then stepping back again across the rope with the left foot and bringing the right foot back to the left foot. On command this pattern is reversed along the length of the rope, starting from both left and right sides. After the child has completed this series of floor-level exercises, more complicated exercises may be devised. For example, he might proceed up and down stairs sideways, to the left and also to the right, in order to help develop both vertical and horizontal laterality.

The next segment is to have the child react to verbal commands, such as putting the left foot forward and raising the left hand on command. These exercises should be done very slowly and routinely in the beginning. When the child begins to develop a better sense of laterality, commands can be speeded up and alternated. Again, it is unwise to push for speed too soon, and confusion should be avoided at all costs, as this may cause a regression in the child's sense of laterality.

Throughout all laterality practices, the child should be encouraged to repeat the directions as he performs the action. The teacher says, "Move the left foot"; the child moves his left foot saying simultaneously, "Move the left foot." The teacher says, "Move the right arm"; the child moves the right arm and says, "Move the right arm." This is a valuable reinforcement for the development of laterality.

TACTILE DISCRIMINATION

TACTILE DISCRIMINATION is the perception or identification of a tangible object by the sense of touch. Because of convenience and ease, the hands are used most for tactile-discrimination practice in the classroom. This does not, however, rule out the use of other parts of the body as tactile receptors.

Tactile-discrimination training begins with large-object identification; reduc-

---

[4] N. C. Kephart, *The Slow Learner in the Classroom* (Columbus, Ohio: Charles E. Merrill, 1966). p. 138.

tion of the size of objects follows gradually. Objects of simple design are presented first and objects of more complicated design are introduced later. Objects can be both identified and matched.

Materials may be selected which differ in weight, texture, substance, and size, and which have various degrees of coldness or warmth.

• The sequence for discriminating weight should start with large, heavy objects as opposed to small, light objects. A large object which weighs as much as five pounds is picked up, while a variety of much smaller objects, such as a pen, ruler, notebook, pillow, etc., are lifted to compare weights. Gradually, objects of nearly the same weight are introduced, calling for more effort in discrimination. At no time should the discriminations become so difficult or so minimal as to put undue stress on the child. It is better to retain the possibility of a correct response by the child at all times.

• Texture discriminations start from coarse materials, such as sandpaper, and are compared to desk-top surfaces, paper, glass, etc. Children can rank, in order of smoothness or roughness, such items as sandpaper, other types of paper, cloth, wood, etc.

• Substance discrimination, such as hardness and softness, can begin by comparing a rock to cotton, cloth, a sponge, or a marshmallow. (The child is allowed to eat the marshmallow.) As a child develops more tactile discrimination, differences in hardness-softness are reduced until he may begin to have difficulty in differentiation. The process should stop at this point. The process of discrimination should be started with the eyes open and proceed to repetition of the same series of identifications with the eyes closed.

• The use of objects of various sizes is one of the most fertile areas to work in for developing tactile discrimination. The child first completes a sequence of touching objects of various sizes and deciding which are larger-smaller, longer-shorter, wider-narrower. The same objects may then be hidden behind a screen, placed in a sack, or touched in the dark, so that the visual sense is not employed.

• Hot and cold discrimination is of lesser importance in tactile training, and outside of calling attention to the fact that hot and cold represent opposites — and the world is full of opposites, such as left-right, tall-short — not much time needs to be devoted to this form of discrimination. A child might profit from trying to identify (in the classroom or outdoors) which objects are holding heat or losing heat easily. The explanation of what causes the sensation of cold or hot should precede the children's exploration.

RHYTHM

EFFECTIVE, rhythmic, neurological serial systems are readily perceived if one watches a skilled athlete perform. Muscles work smoothly together to make it appear that the athlete is almost floating across the ground. A. R. Luria refers to this type of action as a result of " . . . the creation of consecutive series of motor stereotypes, or 'kinetic melodies,' without which skilled movements are impossible."[5]

---
[5] Luria, *op. cit.*, p. 41.

SENSORY-MOTOR

Where rhythm is concerned, there is a close connection between sensory-motor procedures and auditory processes. It is generally felt that rhythms should vary in speed; it would probably be best to start exercises with a slow rhythm, gradually increasing to a faster rhythm. If drawing is done in rhythm on the chalkboard, it should be done in circular form, avoiding angles. Drawing may be done to the accompaniment of music, voice cadence, or a beat drummed by the teacher.

Drummed rhythms in regular patterns are helpful to a child's development. At first, single sides of the body should be employed, either hand or foot reacting to the rhythm, then changing to the opposite side of the body. The next change is to bilateral rhythms which involve motor patterns alternating between the left and right side of the body.

There are two types of rhythm to which a child may respond. With the first type he is able to adjust to the rhythm as he feels it. He could jump up and down, count out loud, clap to music, or even dance about to a tune. The second rhythm is one to which the child is compelled to adjust by the device or nature of the mechanism on which the child is performing. One of these devices is the trampoline; the child has to adjust his jumping to the resilience of the deck. Another example is rope jumping, where the rhythmic pace is set by the other children twirling the rope. The pogo stick is another device, the spring regulating the reciprocal motor movement.

Educationally handicapped children often have difficulty in adjusting to rhythmic rope jumping; therefore, it is best sometimes not to rotate the rope in a complete circle at first. Let the rope be swung back and forth on the ground, with the child jumping over it as it comes toward him from either direction. The next step would be to swing it to and fro slightly off the ground as he jumps over it. Next, swing the rope in a quarter arc, progressing to half a circle. Finally, the rope is swung in a full circle, where the child must anticipate when the rope will pass under his feet. During his jumping he may be asked to say rhymes or jump to the rhythm of verses chanted by those turning the rope. Again, the pattern of jumping would be for the child first to jump with both feet together, then on one foot, on the other foot, and finally, we would progress to the bilateral or alternating foot-jumping pattern. There is a possibility of extending this process to other intricate patterns of jumping, but this demands a higher degree of skill and probably should only be attempted by those who are able to obtain a fine rhythmic sense.

Matching of sounds or rhythmic patterns which are tapped out by the teacher is good practice; however, rhythms should follow simple, straight tapping patterns. Patterns can be done to the accompaniment of music, first playing in straight four-quarter time, then advancing to two-quarter- and three-quarter-time signatures. It is best that the tapping be done on instruments which make clear, crisp sounds that can be differentiated readily without echoing, rather than on those which cause a reverberation.

DIRECTION

AFTER A CHILD has located his own body in space and developed the correct usage of the left and the right sides of his body, he is ready to utilize his body outwardly. Jean Piaget states:

The perceptual space of the small child is less structured along horizontal and vertical coordinates than that of the adult, because such structuring presupposes the establishment of relationships between the object perceived and points of reference siutated at distances beyond the boundaries of the figures. With increasing age, there is a constantly broader and more far-reaching frame of reference as a function of the establishment of perceptual relations. This leads to an ever-increasing qualitative contrast between horizontals and verticals. The error with respect to the vertical line is no doubt due to a difference in the distribution of the points of concentration and of "encounters" on the vertical and on the horizontal lines. The upper and lower parts of the vertical line are not symmetrical from the perceptual point of view (the top is "open" while the bottom is "closed" toward the base), whereas the two halves of the horizontal line are perceptually symmetrical. The small child's space is less structured along coordinates, because his perceptual activity is not concerned with distant relationships. He is thus less sensitive to the qualitative difference between horizontal and vertical lines and to the perceptual asymmetry of the latter, since this asymmetry is a function of the general background of the figure.

In sum, in addition to the "primary" effects which stem from the law of relative contrations, there is a whole body of perceptual activities — transports, comparisons at a distance, transpositions, anticipations, etc. — which, in general, lead to the attenuation of primary errors but can provoke secondary errors when they relate elements at a distance giving rise to contrasts, etc. In other words, they give rise to illusions which would not be produced with the establishment of distant relationships.[6]

Development of the concept of direction in children starts with the child's outward movement from his own midline. The first exercises are with objects within his immediate grasp. The child is then directed to an object or point in space. He may be requested to walk to his left toward the door or to the right to the teacher's desk; directions are issued for frontward and backward movement. Compass points may be placed on plaques or painted on the floor and the child may be directed to walk to designated compass points. The same plaques may be put on outside areas set according to the lines of the compass and he may again be asked to move to specific points. This is similar to a popular television-show game where buried treasures are found at certain points after following compass-point directions. The third stage is when the child is requested to bring faraway objects back to a central point or station from which the child is functioning. Following this achievement level, the child may be asked to perform certain tasks accompanied by another child. Both will then be asked to perform parallel tasks, and it should be pointed out to the children that there are parallel relationships between the two tasks. Lastly, the children may be instructed in how to use crossing pathways, where one child moves into an area that the other has vacated.

---

[6] Jean Piaget, *Six Psychological Studies* (New York, N.Y.: Random House, 1967), pp. 140-141.

SENSORY-MOTOR

MAKING directional movements on chalkboards is a beginning step in directionality which is necessary in reading and writing. The next step would be to use templates and have the child trace (with finger, chalk, or crayon) various simple geometric designs of triangles, squares, and rectangles. The first templates should be constructed at plate size, the second set at saucer size, and the third set at cup size.

The popular game of drawing pictures from numbers is also good following work with the templates. The child draws successive lines from numbers one, two, three, etc. If the child is too young to follow the number sequence successfully the successive numbers may be pointed out to him.

It is suggested that while the child is engaged in these activities he repeat the teacher's directions aloud, in order to reinforce the learning. The child would say, if he were asked to draw a circle to the right, "I'm going to draw a circle to to the right," or, "I am drawing a circle to the right." In the more advanced stages, children may move colored blocks into designated areas according to left-right and up-and-down instructions. After simple proficiency has developed, the child may be helped to construct simple diagrams of the school building and then maps of local areas in the community so that he can see where he lives and studies in relationship to home and school. Field trips can be taken using these maps as guides.

Another profitable way of developing the concept of direction, which is related to the left-to-right coding necessary in the reading process, is found in the neurological-impress method of remedial reading.[7] The neurological-impress method utilizes the teacher's finger going across the page in a left-to-right direction as the child and teacher read aloud together. Later, the teacher holds the child's finger and moves it across the paper. This automatizing of the left-to-right reading direction many hundreds of times helps establish an eye-patterning directionality and aids in smoothing out the reading process.

The same technique can be used in arithmetic with children who have directionality difficulties. For example, in adding columns, the children would be encouraged to run their fingers down the columns going from the right column to the left — which, of course, is a violation of the left-to-right coding of normal reading. In subtraction, they would start on the right side, placing the finger on the top number and moving it downward. In the case of new math (which is recommended since it does not involve working against the left-to-right coding of reading), they would move from the left side of the equation to the right.

TIME SENSE

TIME is one of the least understood of the sensory-motor experiences. At best, time sense seems to move along a continuum as we age. We are all familiar with the oldster and his stories of the past. For the beginning school child, there appears to be much of the present. John H. Flavell states:

> The time of the young infant is most probably a practical time . . .

---

[7] R. G. Heckelman, "Using the Neurological-Impress Remedial-Reading Technique," *Academic Therapy Quarterly*, I (Summer 1966), 235.

(e.g., be brings hand to mouth before sucking, hears the sound before turning to look at the source, etc.), but there is no reason to suspect that the infant himself has any impression of before and after, now and later, etc. As Piaget puts it, a sequence of perceptions does not necessarily imply a perception of sequence. What does the child experience in the temporal domain? Piaget guesses that it is a vague feeling of duration imminent in his own actions, a feeling intermixed with other similarly vague sensations of effort, need, and the like.[8]

When the child reaches school age, a past has begun to be developed and there are beginnings of thought directed toward looking into the future.

Time appears to be most closely related to space. As a prelude to understanding the functions of time, which is divided spatially by clocks, three simple colors may be employed: blue representing past, red indicating present, and green indicating future. Children should be encouraged to work with these three-color patches or three-colored objects in practice sessions. They may be given directions such as, "Place the blue color where you were sitting; put the red color where you are now; and in a few more minutes go across the room to the board and place the green color there." Simple color combinations should be established which relate to these three periods of time and no change of color should be made. Many such experiences should be carried on so they are able to connect the past, present, and future.

A calendar may be used on which the date is identified by the color scheme. Red would indicate the present day, green would be tomorrow's date, and blue would be the past date. The child should change the color system each day.

Sustained musical tones may be employed and the differentiation between long tones and short tones pointed out. The children are asked to move only as long as they can hear the sound.

In general, children's experiences in time help to identify and relate their body to the temporal and spatial world around them and also to the understanding of their own physical position in the world.

REACTION

MOTOR REACTION to auditory directions helps to develop the functioning of two neural systems. The first system involves the capacity to understand or interpret instructions, the other to translate this understanding into a specified form of motor action.

Begin with a one-idea, short sentence, such as "John, stand up." Use only the minimum amount of words necessary in the instructions. The child will be further helped if he repeats the teacher's instructions verbatim: "John, stand up." He then answers while still standing, "I am standing up."

The teacher may add to the learning situation with a multisensory approach by projecting the writing of the instructions on an overhead projector at the same time she is verbalizing the command.

---

[8] John H. Flavell, *The Developmental Psychology of Jean Piaget* (New York, N.Y.: D. Van Nostrand, 1965), p. 147.

SENSORY-MOTOR

The first series of instructions should involve walking, running, or other tasks that utilize larger parts of the body and are part of gross-motor activity. Once success is achieved in these areas, the activity may be narrowed down to fine-motor activity. Once success is achieved in these areas, the activity may be narrowed down to fine-motor activity, such as asking for prescribed hand movements, stacking blocks, arranging objects into patterns, or combinations of divergent activities involving more than one motor system.

After these activities are successfully accomplished, the instructions should include two ideas within the sentence and should call for a two-action response. For example, "John, stand up and turn around." Again, the child repeats the teacher's instructions by saying, "John, stand up . . . and turn around." (His speech should coordinate with the specified action.)

After the child is able to comply with double instructions which call upon diversified motor systems, he then is given extended instructions which involve as many multiple instructions as he is able to carry successfully in his memory. A more complicated process would include sentences that contain phrases and clauses, although instructions of this type should, if possible, be avoided in all areas of sensory-motor training.

No activity should be suggested to the child that causes him to have to think for excessive lengths of time before he starts to carry out the instructions. The goal is to develop a correct instantaneous reaction and to train the child to extend the memory patterns and to utilize all parts of his body in space.

I HAVE ATTEMPTED, in a small way, to outline a large and complicated remedial program. I suggest that sensory-motor sequencing activities are a logical part of a multisensory approach to helping children with educational deficiencies based upon neurological deficits or malfunctions. We need to view motor-training activities as a part of a total program of rehabilitation or development, but we should also be aware that this approach may be overworked and is often advanced as a preventative or "cure-all" for learning disabilities. Teachers often try to implement these activities without fully understanding the three basic postulates:

• Perceptual-motor functions develop through steps of sequential maturation.

• There are identifiable areas of perceptual-motor dysfunction which reflect underlying central-nervous systems mechanisms.

• Both maturation and central-nervous-system integrative functions depend upon appropriate stimulation and response.[9]

In the past, it was believed that children with learning problems got sufficient motor-activity training from permissive play activity; however, modern research tends to point out the need for controlled, specifically directed motor activities. Hence, there is the need to arrange sensory-motor activities in a sequential pattern.

---

[9]W. Elliott, "The Perceptual-Motor Development Project; Title III, ESEA Project: of Sensorimotor Dysfunction in Primary School Children," *Perceptual-Motor Newsletter* (June 1968).

Integrating Form Perception

Floria Coon-Teters

PERCEPTION is a resultant. It represents the sum of many experiences in which the individual has participated, the developmental stage in which the individual finds himself, the condition of the perceptual apparatus, and the integration of that perceptual system with other systems of the organism.

In the case of visual form perception, the primary concern is with the integration of the visual and tactual systems. The expression used most frequently to describe the functioning level of integration of these two systems is "visual motor coordination." The coordination of these two systems is tremendously important for school success. It is basic to reading, writing, spelling, and arithmetic tasks. The ability to perceive forms is a prerequisite to symbol manipulation and symbol interpretation — manually and ideationally.

As described in an earlier article, the optic imagination develops from indistinct vortical movement, with vague color impressions, to loops, ellipses, circles, and finally to distinct crossings, angles, and definite shapes of all varieties moving from the diffuse to the gestalt of objects.[1] Development through the various stages from primitive to complete experiences requires the process of active reality testing.

It is via the active-reality testing that the retinal image, which is two dimensional and consists of juxtapositional patches of sensation, is changed into a three-dimensional construct.

It is accepted more and more among educators that difficulty with symbol recognition or retention will make the educative process difficult. Frequently the decision that a problem exists in the perceptual area is based upon the reproduction which the child makes of some visual stimulus presented to him in the classroom or test situation. While it is not necessarily true that a perceptual problem exists when the child is not able to draw the form correctly, it is true that incorrectly executed figures and forms will feed back incorrect data so that development of accurate form perception will be difficult. What basically may be a motor problem may become a cognitive problem if not corrected.

In examining what might be done for a child who exhibits perceptual problems, the single most important question to be answered is: Is the task untimely? By untimely, it is meant that the child may not be developmentally ready. He

---

[1] Floria Coon, "A Developmental View of Children's Learning," *Academic Therapy*, I (Summer 1966), 220 ff.

may not yet have control of special hand movements required to perform the task. He may not have a feel for the kind of muscle action required. Before beginning any procedures with children, it is advisable to develop a perspective of what is developmentally correct for him. The teacher and other significant adults in the educational settings need to be clear about developmental stages, the relationship of these stages to cognitive development, and the variations in the development between the various systems. It is not uncommon to find that there is a good deal of variability in the various systems during early childhood. It is expected that few of the systems will be fully integrated. True integration of the physiological systems does not take place until young adulthood is reached and a stable personality pattern begins to be demonstrated.

In adolescence, for example, we frequently see systems that appeared to be integrated become disintegrated under the stress of hormonal changes. Often, the difficulties which adolescents encounter in the learning situation are manifestations of the compensations they made earlier for lag in one or more of the perceptual systems.

In the early years, if we permit the child to have experiences which he can handle without too great frustration and with firm, warm guidance, we can make the oscillations and the indecisiveness of growth less traumatic.

It may be that we are more aware of the difficulties today; it may be that the demands upon children are becoming unrealistic in the early school years; or perhaps we have forgotten the wide range of variations in development of the young. Whatever the reasons, it is with increasing frequency that we find perceptual difficulties among our young.

WHAT FOLLOWS is a descriptive account of an approach used with a small group of children who evidenced perceptual difficulties and the results of this approach. It may provide some guidelines for action for those who are concerned with remediation in this particular area.

In screening the children who were to participate, a large number of guidance-department referrals were examined. Rounding out the percentages, it should be noted that 20 percent of the children easily could be classed as slow-developing children; 5 percent had severe and multiple physical problems; 25 percent had special motor and self-concept problems related to the motor problems; one or both of the parents of 35 percent of the children were severely disturbed, or there were major medical problems in the home which proved to be too much for the child. The children with whom we are concerned in this report came from the remaining 15 percent. These children demonstrated some of the characteristics of the educationally handicapped child; i.e., neurological signs that did not appear to be hard signs, mild hyperactivity, inattention, etc.

The two boys and two girls included in this report were in their tenth year. Their teachers felt that the children had greater potential than was being demonstrated in their school work and other activities. The parents were known to the school staff as cooperative, and no family pathology was known to exist. Medical and developmental histories obtained from both the parents and the pediatricians did not show gross problems. Social development in all cases was retarded. The children had various phobias — food, animals, noises — and they were unmotivated.

The psychological batteries showed the following common profiles: All were within the high-average range, had gaps in learning, and showed variations in significant proportions between and within subtests. The children could identify but could not accurately reproduce figures. Distortions of visual memory were present in the tasks. There was greater distortion the longer the exposure time. For example, when figures were exposed to the children for five minutes, their reproductions showed fewer distortions than when the figures were exposed for ten or more minutes prior to the reproductive task.[2] Fine-motor control, eye-hand coordination, kinesthesis of the directions of movement, difficulty in following directions, distorted reality contact were the other common problems indicated.

All of the children became highly anxious when required to carry out directions which required using their body in space. Timed tasks intensified the anxiety and, in one instance, provoked tears and withdrawal.

All four children attended the same school but were in different classrooms. The work with the children was to be done twenty minutes a day, three times a week. The class in which one of the children was enrolled instituted the program introduced by G.N. Getman and E.R. Kane, so one of the four children received double doses of work.[3]

With the help of several teachers, special geometric forms were made. There were two- and three-dimensional representations, in various sizes and shapes, of the geometric forms. The sizes ranged from one inch to forty-eight inches. It was possible for the children to get inside the forty-eight-inch forms and explore from another perspective. The two-dimensional figures of this size were placed on the floor and walls of the classroom. The children explored them with their arms, legs, bodies; walked them (sometimes on all fours), crawled them, danced them. The figures of different sizes were taken outside to the playground and the children perceived them from various distances and angles. Discussion of perception at the different distances and angles took place at all times. Slits and holes were made in filing cards and the children peered at the forms through these apertures. This was exciting for them. They experimented with their fingers and rolled up sheets of paper.

Each child experienced the figures from different angles and was asked to make reproductions of the figures as they appeared from the various views. The differences in the views were shared and explained. Each child knew what we were trying to do and what we hoped to accomplish — improvement in his reading and writing skills. Some children progressed more rapidly than did others. When one child made an advance — for example, when he could join the lines of the corner of a triangle correctly — he discussed with the other children how he had accomplished this and then assisted them in accomplishing the same task.

The children felt the geometric forms with their eyes open, with their eyes blindfolded, or with the objects behind them. They were asked to draw what they felt, dance what they felt, and demonstrate the shapes with their arms.

---

[2] Figures used were from Lauretta Bender's *Visual Motor Gestalt Test* (New York, N.Y.: American Orthopsychiatric Association, 1946).

[3] G. N. Getman and E. R. Kane, *The Physiology of Readiness* (Minneapolis, Minn.: Programs to Accelerate School Success, 1964).

Sketches of the human body were pinned on the wall and the amazing way in which the body is proportioned was demonstrated. The relationship of part-to-part was noted. It was seen that the body parts may be viewed as triangles, rectangles, cones, spheres, etc. The children drew the body abstractly, using geometric forms.

As the children demonstrated development of kinesthetic direction of movement and comprehension of basic forms, games were introduced which required eye-hand movements. At the same time each child was assigned a job as a "teacher's helper." The job for each was to make ditto copies of work prepared by a teacher. This work was for distribution to children in classes other than the child's own. Directions for the work were printed out by the teacher, and the child was required to check off each step as he completed it. This caused him to work slowly and safely, following guidance. Each child had the opportunity to assist in the following areas: spelling, arithmetic, and poetry. This activity was multipurpose.

• The child began to acquire form perception of the kind needed in the school setting.

• He received exposure to following directions.

• He gained experience in presenting the materials appropriately.

He experienced alleviation of anxiety in the learning situation while being exposed to academic information.

• The child later corrected the papers in arithmetic and spelling.

AT THE END of sixteen weeks, three of the children demonstrated gains. The child who had burst into tears and withdrawn under the stress of timed tasks in the testing situation became compulsive about drawing and school work. He was inordinately neat and took hours to accomplish relatively simple tasks.

The three who showed the desired results demonstrated the following gains: Bender and Memory for Designs reproductions were above average.[4] Differences between and within tests were diminished. Improvement in fine-motor control and eye-hand-coordination was demonstrated in day-to-day classwork. These children were better able to follow directions and to respond appropriately and correctly. More initiative in the classroom situation was demonstrated. Teachers described them as active but not hyperactive, and as participating more freely in physical education and other school activities. Academically, their papers were neater and more accurate, words were spelled accurately with fewer number of trials, handwriting improved, and the average reading gain was 1.3 grade points.

Parents of these three children noted that the children were socializing more, were pleasanter, were less clumsy (particularly at the dinner table), were more willing to go to school, and talked more about school and school friends.

The children who were in the classroom where the Getman techniques were used were described as having made similar types of progress. In particular, this class had fewer behavior problems according to the principal. The child who was

---

[4] Bender, *op. cit.*; Frances K. Graham and Barbara S. Kendall, *Memory for Designs Test* (Missoula, Mont.: Psychological Test Specialists, 1946).

exposed to both the class and the special sessions made the greatest gains. The greatest gains for her were in the areas of social competence, self-image and capacity to discuss future goals.

ALL FOUR CHILDREN were described as having progressed greatly in the area of communication skills. The capacity to focus one's attention on what is being said is often dependent on whether what is being said has relevance or is understandable. The capacity to participate is dependent on whether one feels able to do that which the activity requires. Many words are understood first through experiencing and "muscle feel." It is interesting to observe how often a passive child has difficulty with verbs or with time concepts. The handling of time and the comprehension of verbs requires a perception of form. Almost every discipline requires a perception of form. The process of development is not linear but spiral. It requires many gross-motor activities with accurate feedback, many fine-motor activities with accurate feedback, and the integration of these motor activities with other systems. Cognitive development, the "logical maps," the organization of thought, and the projection of oneself in time and space depend on the child's experiences. The form perceptions which result from these experiences directly affect the child's capacity to succeed in school.

The work reported here and similar work done in this area — concentrating on the physiological needs of the child and not attacking specific academic areas — suggests that schools might find it more productive to focus on the physiological and psychological prerequisites for learning before deciding that the child has a learning problem.

Learning is satisfying for its own sake as well as having value as a tool. Each child originally brings to school eagerness, curiosity, a desire to find out. It is the task of the teacher to draw out, not to pour in, to set the stage for the inquiring mind, to create a learning situation which will invite the explorer, unafraid. It is the responsibility of all teachers to teach in such a manner that avenues to learning are opened, not closed. Even more challenging in this respect is the task of the remedial teacher who must re-open avenues closed by fear and self-doubt resulting from repeated failure.

— **Dorothy S. Blackmore, Ed.D.**
"Preparing Teachers for the
   Educationally Handicapped,"
Academic Therapy Quarterly, I
(Fall 1965).

Building Patterns of Retention

Harold B. Helms

JIMMY finished working with his set of flashcards. Yes, he knew every one of the words in the pack. He had gone through them several times. The teacher then gave him a primer which contained most of the words in the set of flashcards. Jimmy started the first line: "How is there?" The teacher said, "Jimmy, that first word is *who* — not *how*. We just learned it on the flashcards." And so Jimmy continued on down the page with his hit-and-miss approach to the words he had "learned" a short time earlier.

Anne had studied her spelling words with her mother all week long. On the night before the weekly spelling test, she reviewed the words several times. When she left home Friday morning, both she and her mother were confident that this week, at long last, she would score 100 percent on the test. Anne took her test — and missed half of the words.

Johnny sat at his desk copying a paragraph which his teacher had written on the chalkboard. The teacher walked around the room checking the work of the children. She saw Johnny's paper. The letters were spread up and down on the line, words were missing, and entire lines were left out.

These three examples of academic behavior are common characteristics observed in some of the children in every classroom. In clinical-remedial situations and in classrooms, the children do not appear to be able to retain information at the symbolic level. This is just one of the many problems experienced by bright children who have learning problems.

To better grasp what is happening as these children attempt to learn, we should look back upon the process of growth and development. We should also think about the nature of words: What are they? Words are abstractions of experiences expressed in an agreed-upon method of communication. In addition to being abstractions, they are also generalizations. For example, the word *clothes* stands for an entire category of items with certain defined characteristics. The word *shirt* is more specific, although it may still be included in the general category of *clothes*. To become still more specific, we might refer to *the blue shirt* or *the shirt with the button missing*. These items are still clothes, of course, but the communication has now moved to a more precise and sophisticated level of abstraction. The fact that we are able to generalize is one of the conditions that makes communication possible.

As children grow they learn to express their needs in the same mode as that of their closest associates — the family group. This shaping of the vocal apparatus takes place in the presence of auditory stimulation and patterning. The little child sees (or experiences) a large, yellow vehicle with many windows. It is called "bus." The abstractive process permits the child to experience an orange or red or blue vehicle with the same general characteristics, and yet, to the child, it is still a "bus." For some children who seem to have had sufficient experience at the motor-generalization level this process of extension to the perceptual-cognitive level is not a problem. After one or two experiences with a form (such as a bus), the child can make the appropriate vocal-auditory-abstractive association. Some other children seem to need more than one or two exposures to the stimulus to make the proper association.

This same type of abstractive ability — requiring cognitive processing, memory, and generalization — is needed for words just as much as it is needed for concrete experiences. Symbolic growth, however, is built on the base of rich perceptual and motor development. Since other chapters in this compilation deal with these factors, they will not be covered here, save to reiterate their importance to the academic performance of the child.

When children experience and demonstrate the types of disabilities manifested by Jimmy, Anne, and Johnny, spelling the words over and over or working with the flashcards over and over is not the answer — as teachers and therapists will readily agree. What is needed is a program which will build into the child the ability to retain and use the symbolic material and to make the appropriate shifts from one form of presentation to another.

The activities suggested here should coincide with other aspects of a total program. Teachers and therapists will want to assure themselves that the problem does not rest in a visual- or auditory-acuity problem or in a discrimination problem. Testing by the proper visual and auditory specialists, the school nurse, and the district psychologist will help in ruling out specific but subtle problems in these areas.

The activities, with the proper modifications, can be used with younger as well as with older children. The principles and the sequences, however, should remain basically the same.

A PROGRAM for building retention should utilize the major channels of learning — tactile-kinesthetic, auditory, and visual. Since tactile-kinesthetic organization and development have been presented elsewhere in this compilation, the major emphasis here will be on the auditory and visual levels of integration.

Young children should have many experiences in manipulating a variety of objects. Manipulations of this type should offer them the opportunity to grasp, handle, and finally order objects in their environment. For example, *big* and *little*, *front* and *back*, *top* and *bottom*, *in* and *out*, *flat* and *round*, and so on, are important concepts which are learned first in relation to the body and then transferred to the space world; finally they are used in manipulating two-dimensional objects — such as marks on the page that stand for words.

As children handle objects, the teacher should encourage them to say, "Which is bigger?" or, "Which weighs more?" The emphasis should be on gross differences at first, and if the child is having serious retention problems, only two objects should be compared at a time. All other stimuli which might prove distracting should be removed from the teaching-learning area. At first nonmanipulable objects should be used. Two children might be compared: "Who is taller, Jimmy or Johnny?" "Is Johnny shorter or taller than the window sill?" The switch should then be made to manipulative objects. One might, for example, introduce two spools — one large, one small. The child might be asked, "Which is bigger?" A paperweight and a ball might be used next, asking the child, "Which weighs more?" Practice should continue at this level until the teacher feels confident that the child can discriminate between two objects at these sensory levels.

A similar approach should also be used with tones. The children can assist the teacher in constructing a sound table which includes objects that make various sounds when they are struck. The children can take turns in striking two objects in sequence and then asking the others, "Which was the louder — the ball or the can?" An even more simple sound-discrimination exercise is for a child to clap his hands and have his turn at asking, "Which was softer — the first or the second?"

A variation to the discrimination training described above is to have the children close their eyes and describe what they hear or feel. Such activities help them to develop the ability to visualize or picture what is around them when they must depend upon sensory clues other than their ability to see.

The next stage in the sequence is to move from two objects only to a series of objects. The basic principle is to provide the child with opportunities to make more total decisions based on sorting and grouping similar and dissimilar objects. The danger is that it can easily become "busy work" — which leads to boredom and resentment. A way to avoid this reaction is to introduce the tasks on a self-competitive basis. The child seems to gain an understanding that something more than "Just doing" it is involved if one takes the approach, "Let's see if you can do it faster this time," or, "Let's see how many you can do in three minutes."

The first type of sorting should be on the basis of color differentiation. Any number of objects — and any variety — may be used. For example, if the child is sorting jar lids, he should have only lids in his sorting tray. If he is sorting discs, there should be only discs. He should be told exactly what he is to do. "Today, let's see if you can take out only the red discs"; or, "Today, let's take out only the small discs."

If the child is successful, and the process is readily understood and accomplished, then establish two criteria. "Today, take out only the large red discs." Some children will easily handle one direction, but two may prove difficult, so provide a picture-guide for the child. "This is what I want you to remove from the tray. You can look at this picture of a large red disc whenever you want." Of course, the child who needs to continually check against the picture will need to have varied experiences at this level.

As the child becomes successful in handling the process at this stage, additional difficulties should be added. For example, if the child is working with buttons, a wide variety should be included in the box — big ones, little ones, fat ones, thin ones, red ones, yellow ones, and so on.

SENSORY-MOTOR

The child should be encouraged to verbalize at all stages of this procedure. Ask him, "What are you going to do?" Encourage him to describe in his own words just what he is doing. Ask him in many different ways what he is doing: "Today we'll sort these," or, "Today, group the red ones," and so on.

MOST CHILDREN, after sufficient experience, will be able to move from the concrete to the abstract, thus continuing to build a wide variety of percepts. The following criterion should be used by the teacher: Does the child grasp the concept of alike and different at gross concept levels when the range of differences is controlled? Sound judgment on the part of the teacher is necessary in making this decision. The speed with which the child responds to the activities and his ability to explain what he is doing are important indicators for making the transition.

I have found that an excellent way of making the transition is to prepare like and different objects on pieces of heavy-duty cardboard (five inches by twelve inches is a good hand size). Buttons, lids, pencils, and so on, can easily be glued to heavy-duty cardboard, and the pieces of cardboard can be comfortably stored in a large box. (See figure 1.)

Figure 1.

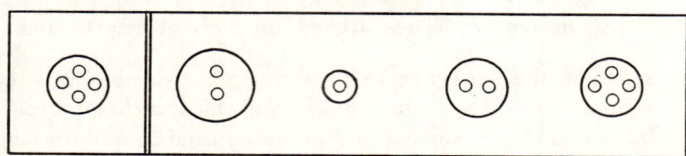

The advantage of this is that one card at a time can be taken from the box and placed before the child. The child is asked, "Which one is exactly the same as the first one?" or, "Which one is just the same as this one?"

If the child moves comfortably through a series of such cards, then add a level of difficulty by saying, "Now look closely. I want you to tell me which one is different from the first one. Don't tell me, though, until I have turned the card over. Is it the second one, the third one, the fourth one, or the fifth one?" Turn the card over then and encourage the child to tell you which one was different in terms of its placement on the board. As you can see, in addition to developing his ability to retain, the child is also developing his ability to sequence. If he has difficulty, let him look at the card again. Some children will be able to select the different one quite easily when looking at the card, but be unable to remember it when the card is removed from view.

Figure 2.

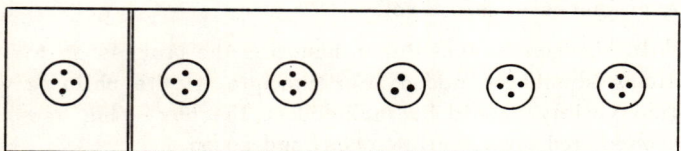

A necessary ingredient to successful teaching, is, of course, to determine where the child functions well and when he begins to have difficulties. When problems arise, the child should be returned to the level at which he was functioning comfortably, and the activities should be gauged to build his abilities at that level by increasing the complexity.

The child should next be given experiences in differentiating forms in which the spatial orientation has been altered. The major difference in this stage is that the activity becomes a totally two-dimensional procedure. Cards are presented on which a number of forms are drawn. (See figure 3.) The form on the left side of the card is the same as one of the other forms, except that it is positioned differently. The child is asked to determine which form is the same as the first one. When he becomes proficient at this, the card can be turned over after he has looked at the forms, and he can be asked to designate from memory (second, third, or fourth) which of the forms was the same as the first.

Figure 3.

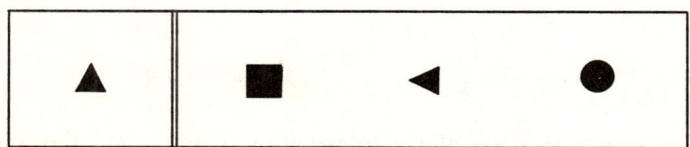

At this stage, when working with young children, ditto sheets may be used. The forms depicted may be basically the same as those shown on the cards. The emphasis should be on accuracy first, and then on speed. Figure 4 illustrates examples of exercises that might be prepared on ditto sheets.

Figure 4.

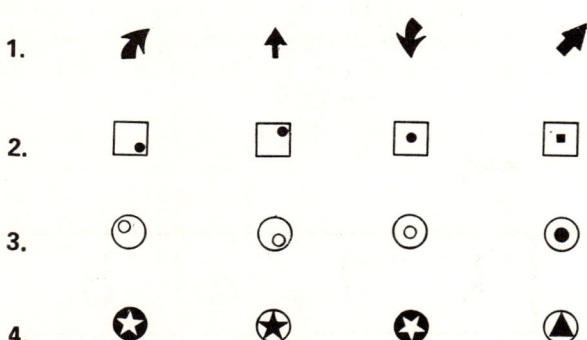

An additional exercise in form and spatial differentiation at a two-dimensional level is to have each child in the class make for display a name card (8½ by 11 inch paper is fine) on which his name is written in several different ways. (See figure 5.)

SENSORY-MOTOR

Figure 5.

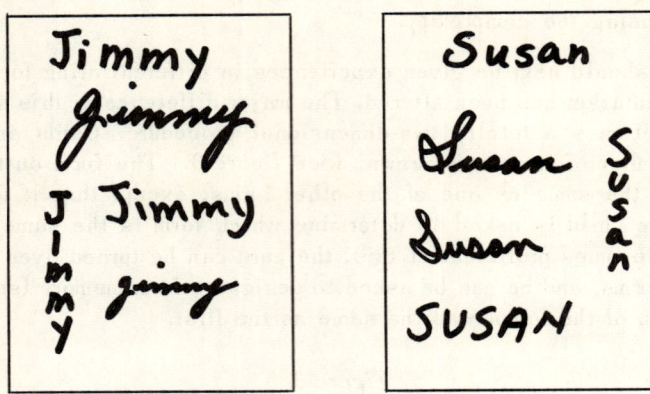

Moving into symbols.

Older youngsters — particularly teenagers — can bypass the activities described in the preceding section. For these children, the emphasis can be placed right away on working with letters and words. For example, the student might be given exercises to help him learn to discriminate differences and likenesses in letter shapes. Figure 6 illustrates, in suggested sequence, exercises that are helpful in building retention at the visual level. Naming the letters should be a subtle, nonstress aspect of the activity. The child would be asked, "Which letter is exactly the same as the first one?" The youngster can be taken through some of the exercises step by step, and specific instructions might have to be given on what is meant by the word "exactly.")

Figure 6.

1. Which is exactly the same

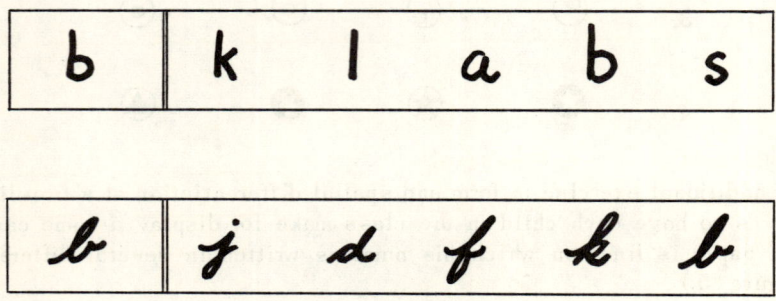

BUILDING PATTERNS

2.

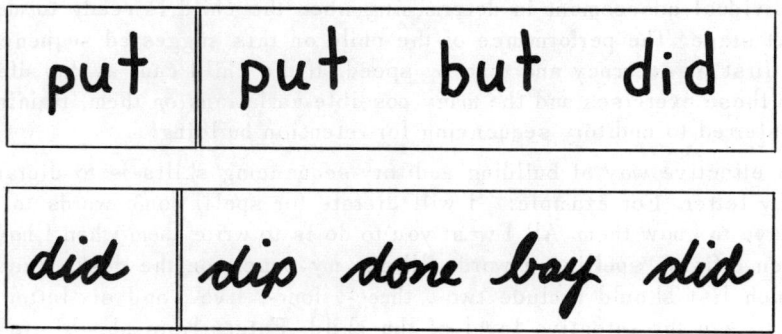

Then the students, with success at this level, are ready to move to identification of likenesses when the form is changed.

1.

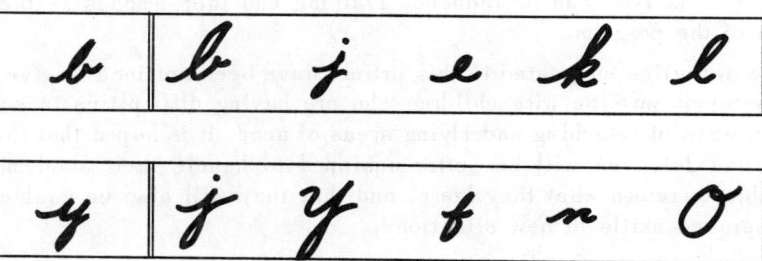

2.

put	dut	*put*	*dot*	pot

did	*dip*	dip	*did*	bid

3.

		Same	Different
See me. run.	See me run.	_____	_____
Look at them.	Look at these.	_____	_____
Open the door.	Open the floor.	_____	_____
Go right now.	Go right now.	_____	_____

25

The teacher or educational therapist will have to use experience, background, and individual assessment in determining when the child is ready to move on to the next stage. The performance of the child on this suggested sequence can be judged first by accuracy and then by speed. If the child can, at the silent level, perform these exercises and the many possible variations on them, training should be transferred to auditory sequencing for retention building.

An effective way of building auditory-sequencing skills is to dictate words, letter by letter. For example: "I will dictate (or spell) some words to you. You don't have to know them. All I want you to do is to write them when I have finished. When I finish spelling a word, I'll tap my pencil on the desk. Ready?" The first such list should include two-, three-, four-, five-, and six-letter words — simply to see the retentive level of the child. Future lists should gradually include words of greater length. For example, if the child is successful with three-letter words but begins to fail with four- and five-letter words, then the training should be at four letters. Teachers will find that it takes at first a great deal of training, but once the child begins to develop retention at this level, he moves ahead quickly. Once the child is able to retain seven letters in sequence, further training of this type can be reduced. Training can then emphasize the academic aspects of the program.

The activities suggested in this article have been outlined to give the teacher or therapist working with children who are having difficulties in school some possible ways of attaching underlying areas of need. It is hoped that the Jimmies, Annes, and Johnnies will be better equipped to handle their academic work by being able to retain what they learn, and that they will also be enabled to apply their improved skills to new situations.

Hand-Eye Coordination

Shirley H. Linn

WHEN we give an assignment to students, we usually assume that they have already acquired the basic visual-perceptual skills needed to do the task. When a child fails to carry out the task successfully, we seldom question why this occurs. We must learn to ask more questions about the "why" of failure in terms of skills needed for achievement. We must take a long, hard look at the skills involved in carrying out every assignment in the classroom. Most of these skills are directly or indirectly dependent on hand-eye coordination.

Poor hand-eye coordination is one of the many sources of the "why" of classroom failure. It is an integral part of the total schema of human growth and development; it is affected by previous experiences and, in turn, it affects experiences and achievement in the future. When we consider the role of hand-eye coordination in this manner, we can readily see that a developmental lag in this area will seriously affect other areas.

Hand-eye coordination is built on the skills and information that children accrue from the normal daily activities of living and play as they grow and develop from the time of birth. Many children learn these skills without effort. Others do not.

Skills and information essential for hand-eye coordination develop first within the child's own body in terms of the muscle movements he makes as he plays and moves about. In time, each movement and each change in direction must become controlled by a visual stimulus. The child must learn to recognize the stimulus, translate visual recognition into commands from the brain to the muscles, translate nerve impulses received by muscles into movement patterns, and then create new sets of recognitions, messages, and translations based on new stimuli.[1] The child learns to make these associations as he learns to move his body — as he turns over, creeps, crawls, pulls up to his knees and feet, walks, touches, sees, feels, watches his hands move, and manipulates things. All of these activities are essential to the development of hand-eye coordination, and since they should occur before a child reaches school age, we assume he has mastered them by the time he enters school. Often our assumption is incorrect.

---

[1] D.H. Radler and Newell C. Kephart, *Success Through Play* (New York, N.Y.: Harper and Brothers, 1960), pp. 63-65.

SENSORY-MOTOR

As a child grows and develops, hand-eye coordination improves, but the demands for more perfection in its use increases proportionately. As early as kindergarten or preschool nursery, children with hand-eye coordination disturbance encounter difficulty achieving any measure of success in their activities. The first serious problems occur during the transition from preschool nonacademic activities to academic activities in the early grades. By the time the child enters grade school he is expected to have mastered many gross motor-coordination skills, as well as many finer coordination skills.

Training and remediation.

REMEDIATION and training of hand-eye coordination is an ongoing process, part of which is general in nature, and part of which is concerned more specifically with academic subject areas. In general, hand-eye coordination has its roots in gross motor skill and experiences and gradually progresses to the development of finer coordination. Thus, when hand-eye coordination lags, it may be due to a developmental lag in early childhood experiences. Training and remediation for children with poor hand-eye coordination should be organized to anticipate that a "skip" or lag can occur, or has occurred, at any time along the growth and developmental continuum. For this reason, we cannot consider hand-eye coordination an entity in itself; when it is deficient, we must consider it a result of a developmental lag. Motor development, evaluation of motor skills, and remediation of these skills are discussed in detail in publications by Newell C. Kephart, D. H. Radler, and Marianne Frostig.[2] With the information given in these publications and that obtained through the use of the Purdue Perceptual-Motor Survey, few questions are left unanswered concerning perceptual-motor development or its remediation and training.[3]

Once a child has begun to achieve in gross motor areas, he should begin to internalize directionality and laterality in order to match information about changes of eye positions with changes of body position. He should begin to develop better control over his muscles, and gradually his coordination should progress from large to small muscles. By so doing, his coordination improves from large to small, gross to fine movements.

Many preacademic or nonacademic activities are needed to develop hand and eye coordination before youngsters undertake academic work. Hand and eyes are encouraged to work together through simple activities, such as tearing, cutting, and pasting, as well as by playing with blocks, cars, lick-and-stick books, paper dolls, and puzzles.

As simple as these activities seem, they are formidable and disagreeable tasks for children with a disturbance of hand-eye coordination. Because human beings tend to avoid things which are difficult or which present the possibility of failure, these activities are often avoided by children who have difficulty with them, thus eliminating the opportunity for needed practice.

---

[2] Newell C. Kephart, *The Slow Learner in the Classroom* (Columbus, Ohio: Charles E. Merrill, 1960); Radler and Kephart, *op. cit.*; Marianne Frostig and David Horne, *The Frostig Program for the Development of Visual Perception* (Chicago, Ill.: Follett, 1964).

[3] Eugene G. Roach and Newell C. Kephart, *The Purdue Perceptual-Motor Survey* (Columbus, Ohio: Charles E. Merrill, 1966).

When a child cannot achieve success in these activities, he should be given more assistance, and this requires careful study of the skills needed to achieve success in the activity. A step-by-step presentation of the play-learning task should be given, taking into account the skills needed. Deliberate progression should be made through one level of difficulty to another until the goal has been achieved. It is equally important to withdraw assistance so the child will learn to function independently.

Children with poor coordination of hands and eyes are under pressure to finish their assignments, as are all children. However, because of their disability, they are usually slower and even more pressured for enough time in which to do all of their work. To make matters worse, when they are given remedial help in deficient areas, time is taken from their regular assignments.

This discussion is concerned particularly with hand-eye coordination activities which reinforce the basic academic skills needed early in grade-school experience. These activities serve to develop the necessary coordination, and they also may be utilized to teach the child the academic skills at the beginning level. Without this early mastery of skills, the child will encounter many difficulties later on.

From scribbling to writing.

CHILDREN with a developmental lag in hand-eye coordination often need more experience with scribbling than do most children. A child must learn to watch his hands and to follow and internalize the visual image of the line made by the hand. Finer muscular control results from this achievement. As control is gained, lines which once looked like disconnected, overlapped, meaningless forms take on more meaningful appearances. They become pictures, letters, and symbols which have meaning to their creator. As hand-eye coordination improves, the youngster is able to make lines without watchful attention to every movement, and he learns to use his eyes rather than his hands in keeping the place. Eventually his hand and eye movements are matched accurately enough to enable him to substitute information from his eye that he had previously gained from movement of his hand. Hand-eye coordination precedes eye control and is closely associated with all other areas of visual perception.

Scribbling is traditionally associated with activities of very young children. However, it is important that it be presented to youngsters at the time they need it, regardless of their age. If scribbling activities are disguised in different types of media, they are usually acceptable to any age group. For example, one might introduce sand painting, finger painting, dry tempera on wet paper, chalk drawing, or exercises with colored pencils.

Scribbling is obviously the forerunner of writing. However, children with hand-eye coordination problems are seldom ready for writing immediately following success with scribbling. More structured activities are needed first, and for this purpose the Visual-Motor section of the Frostig Program for the Development of Visual Perception is highly recommended.[4]

---

[4] Frostig and Horne, *op. cit.*

SENSORY-MOTOR

When youngsters have experienced some success with relatively structured exercises, they may be ready for prewriting activities. For children with hand-eye coordination problems, tracing raised letters is often beneficial. The procedure for tracing the letters — that is, the direction of the lines — should be the same as will be used in writing them; this, of course, is dependent upon the writing system that has been selected for the class.

Inexpensive tracing cards can be made from yarn glued onto oak tag. For the beginner, lines of letters should be color-cued to show the difference in the directions of lines. Variegated yarn is useful and economical, since there are many colors on each skein of yarn. If the writing system uses color cues, the colors on the cards should coordinate with it. Color cues, however, should be used only long enough to assure the child's success in this activity. The size of the letters should be determined by the needs of the children, but should progress, as coordination improves, from large to small. The letters should conform to the writing style which has been adopted. Arrows drawn to the sides of letters reinforce the direction of the lines.

Other materials can also be used to make raised letters: glitter sprinkled on lines of glue, paper mache, cornstarch modeling goop, play dough, or modeling clay. Making cards for the use of each student can provide additional reinforcement. After using textured letters, raised letters with less texture can be made by tracing a line of glue along drawn or printed letters. These letters become slightly raised as the glue dries. For children who have difficulty making the transfer from one type of activity to another, letters traced on tagboard with felt markers may be a helpful step.

Another helpful approach is to have the child trace inside the openings left when letters have been cut out of linoleum or shaped out of melted plastic granules. The hand is able to move in the desired direction inside the cutout where there is little structure. This method makes it possible for the teacher to check to see how well the youngster has internalized the directions in which his hand should move in order eventually to make the lines to form letters.

Writing exercises with paper and pencil should follow the tracing activities. Assistance is essential at this stage of progress. Constant supervision is needed to check every line a child makes. It is far easier for these children to make a line go in the wrong direction than it is for them to guide it correctly. Because of this, when left on their own, they often learn incorrectly. The teacher must supplement paper-and-pencil exercises with supervision, verbal directions, and whenever necessary, by putting her own hand over the youngster's hand to guide it. Pointing to the appropriate place for a line to be drawn helps the child to make lines go in the correct direction. Because so many directions are involved, writing is a difficult task for children with hand-eye coordination disturbance.

Spelling.

SPELLING workbooks usually require that children write beginning letters, vowels, endings, and finally, words. The child with problems in hand-eye coordination may have difficulty obtaining the correct information from the directions, but even if he is able to obtain the correct information, he still may be unable to write because of the reasons discussed above. If he is able to write, eye and hand may not work together well enough to enable him to place answers on the correct blank. Visual imagery may be affected and this, in turn, may affect memory of the correct sequence of letters. Many persons with problems in hand-eye coordination can spell orally, but they are unable to write the words. Some may overcome this disability by typing words as they are dictated, but on the other hand, they are lost if they have to watch the keyboard in order to strike the correct letters.

In order for some of these children to learn to write spelling words on paper, they must learn to make an auditory-visual letter match. In this way, they learn to use the stronger auditory areas to build up the weak visual area. To build an auditory-visual match, the child should be exposed simultaneously to auditory and visual stimuli (hearing and seeing the letter symbol). One or the other stimulus is then presented and the youngster is required to make the proper response. Activities can be added which involve choosing the correct symbol to go with a specific visual symbol. As these skills are developed, spelling words may be taught by pointing to each letter as the child says it. With his eyes closed, the child imagines what the letter looks like and then writes it, saying each letter as it is written. The final step is to write the entire word.

Reading.

A LAG in visual-motor coordination affects visual coordination, visual memory, and in general it interferes with the learning of the reading process. Without some degree of visual coordination, reading is difficult, if not impossible. For these reasons and those mentioned previously, children may not see a word as it is presented. They may be unable to look at a word long enough or accurately enough to obtain a clear visual image or to remember it. Instead of obtaining a visual image of the whole word, they may notice only part of it. In attempting to recall the word, they may recall any word with a similar configuration or similar visual clues, the first word learned that has a similar beginning letter, or the most recently learned word which has some similarity.

Children with a disability in hand-eye coordination usually have problems following an object with their eyes. It is difficult for them to follow a line of print from left to right, to return their eyes to the left, or to return their eyes to the correct line on the left when the previous line has been completed.

In the early stages of reading, children point to words as they read. This is an important way of using hands and eyes together in order to keep the place and to strengthen the left-to-right movement which the eyes, independent of the hands, eventually takes over.

It is a frustrating experience when hands and eyes are not working together. If a child cannot point to words as they are read, it is a good indication that he may also be unable to move his eyes in order to keep the place accurately.

In general, the activities mentioned earlier reinforce reading skills. However, teaching reading vocabulary and reading itself can be done in such a manner that hand-eye coordination and visual coordination may also be trained.

SENSORY-MOTOR

By supplementing and enlarging upon the suggestion by Marianne Frostig for using a chart to train left-to-right movement and coordination of eyes, we can also teach some reading skills.[5]

Charts can be made in many different ways. For example, single letters can be spaced apart, then the word formed by the letters can be printed at the end of the same line. (See Figure 1.) The youngster points to each letter as it is said. When the end of the line is reached, the entire word is said with a left-to-right sweep of the hand as indicated by the left-to-right pronunciation of the single sounds blended into the word. This shows the child the blend of the parts into the whole. For a pointer, the child may use his hand, a yardstick, a ruler, or even a flashlight. Whether the child actually says each letter and the resulting word is dependent on how involved he can be in a learning activity before his system overloads and cancels the possible advantages.

Figure 1

d	o	g	dog
c	a	t	cat
h	o	g	hog

Charts can be devised to teach many things, ranging from nonacademic material to complicated syllabication or sentences. They can be as ingenious as the teacher wishes or as her imagination allows.

The approach discussed above, which teaches hand-eye coordination along with writing and reading skills, reaches and remediates many of the greatest problems resulting from hand-eye coordination disturbance. This approach calls the attention of a youngster to the different parts of a word, to differences in configuration, sounds, and letters, then to the final blending of the letters into a whole word. As a result, the child's vocabulary is increased, spelling improves, recognition and recall is stimulated, hands and eyes learn to work together, and later on, the eyes begin to work in a more coordinated manner.

Arithmetic.

COUNTING is the basic skill on which future success in arithmetic depends. Meaningful counting requires an association of the appropriate numeral to a certain number of objects. If hands and eyes are not working together, it is almost impossible to achieve this association. Common problems for children with poor hand-eye coordination include: skipping objects when counting them, or touching one object two or more times while counting only one number. This lack of a basic ability makes a poor background on which to develop a sound understanding of the concepts of the number system.

---

[5] *Ibid.*

HAND-EYE COORDINATION

Activities which require the youngsters' use of hands and eyes provide necessary practice prior to the academic experience with arithmetic. If the children are guided and supervised, activities can be introduced that require hand-eye coordination, as well as teaching it. Such activities might include, for example, sorting the appropriate number of objects, grouping objects, and playing with blocks and matchums.

Unless sound foundations are laid for the appropriate association of symbols with the correct number of objects, concepts in arithmetic will be inaccurate and operations faulty. Simply counting orally is not adequate. The child must be able to pick up, set down, group, or move objects in a manner that enables him to give each object the correct numeral. As he does this, he must be carefully watched and guided.

Pegboards with taped-on number symbols (with the appropriate symbol placed above each hole) assist in making the auditory-hand-eye association correctly, thus avoiding the risk that the child might learn incorrectly. (See Figure 2.)

Figure 2

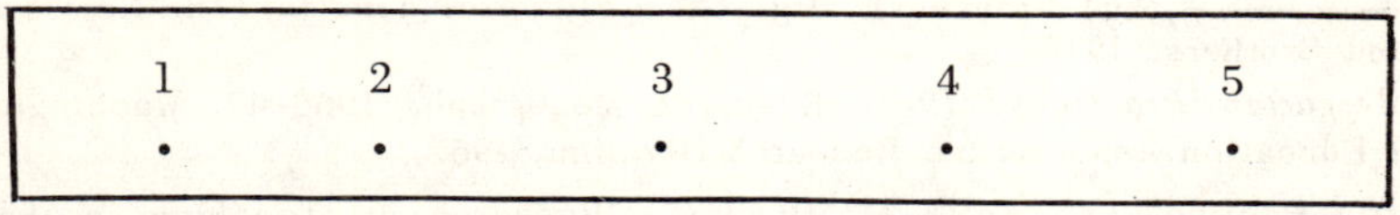

```
┌─────────────────────────────────┐
│  1     2     3     4     5      │
│  •     •     •     •     •      │
└─────────────────────────────────┘
```

Grouping objects is important, but it is often poorly done. As opposed to counting in a one-to-one associative sequence as in the above activity, each group must be counted from the symbol "1." Children often have difficulty making this transfer. Again, pegboards may be used to advantage. Instead of putting numbers along the board in a left-to-right sequence, it is helpful to put them in a vertical sequence. (See Figure 3.)

Figure 3

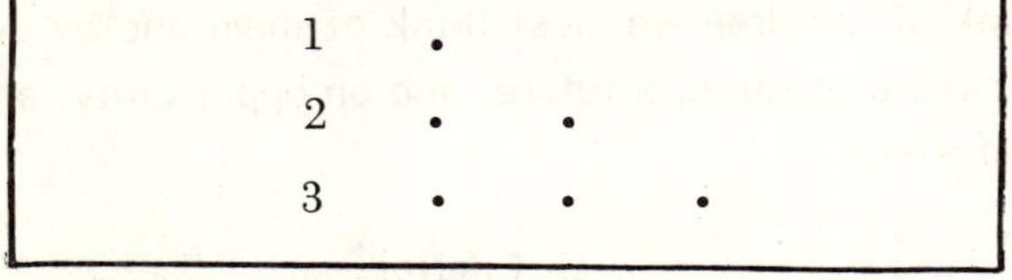

```
┌─────────────────────────┐
│   1   •                 │
│   2   •   •             │
│   3   •   •   •         │
└─────────────────────────┘
```

Another way in which one-to-one association can be developed is to have the youngster draw balls, putting the representative symbol under each illustration as it is completed. In this way, the youngster is building his own number line.

All of the above suggestions can be adapted for adding, subtracting, and other operations of arithmetic. Some children need concrete experience with symbol-object association for a much longer time than do others.

SENSORY-MOTOR

As youngsters progress in school, the print in workbooks, texts, and worksheets becomes smaller and pages become more congested. Students need to learn how to screen out distractions by placing pieces of paper over the part not being used in order to keep the place and to indicate the places in which responses are to be written.

IN CONCLUSION, it is the teachers who must observe, guide, create, and produce as they move along with their students. This requires an understanding of the sequence of skills which are needed by all children. By building into the program opportunities to develop needed skills, the teacher can more effectively help the children. In a short discussion of a vast area, only suggestions can be offered. It is hoped that these suggestions will promote further new ideas for helping the learning-disabled child to overcome his problems.

REFERENCES

Gesell, Arnold, and Catherine Amatruda, *Developmental Diagnosis*. New York, N.Y.: Harper and Brothers, 1948.

——————, and Frances L. Ilg. *The Child from Five to Ten*. New York, N.Y.: Harper and Brothers, 1948.

Kindergarten Practices, 1961. Research Monograph, 1962-M2. Washington, D.C.: National Education Association, Research Division, 1962.

Sears, Pauline, and Edith M. Dowley. "Research on Teaching in the Nursery School," *Handbook of Research on Teaching*. Edited by N.L. Gage. Chicago, Ill.: Rand McNally, 1963.

Standing, E.M. *The Montessori Method*. Fresno, Calif.: Academy Library Guild, 1962.

Wills, Clarice D., and William H. Stegeman. *Living in Kindergarten*. Chicago, Ill: Follett, 1956.

When we speak of children we must think of them one by one remembering that in each case a promise, a future, and an opportunity, and an irreplaceable life is at stake.

— G. Fradier
The Unesco Courier,
(November 1960).

Laterality and Directionality

Sheila Doran Benyon

NEUROLOGICALLY and anatomically we are equipped to view the world through our senses in a two-sided fashion. We possess what is referred to as a midline, an imaginary line that divides us into two distinct halves, which has its origin in the two hemispheres of the brain. Thus, what we do with our right-sided body parts is initiated in the left cortical hemisphere. Through the vertical and horizontal organization of the brain and all the intricate neurological connections contained therein and throughout the body, both sides mesh so that we can function as corporate, organized creatures.

At birth, the majority of us are fully equipped to cope with the complexities of learning. We have the internal mechanisms necessary to process and store the vital information presented to us from the moment of birth. It is through the interpretation of mental movement and sense perceptions that we acquire a true understanding of ourselves and our environment.

Laterality is usually referred to as the internal awareness of the two sides of the body. Laterality is not innate, but rather it is learned through the compilation of sensory and motor data as experienced through the given neurological and anatomical systems.

An infant initiates movement as a sweep of action, completely undifferentiated, and often as a result of basic reflex reactions. By slow deliberate processing, he learns to systematically innervate or inhibit specific muscle groups in order to initiate, sustain, or cease movement on both sides or on one side of his body. In the beginning, balance is his true means to an end in establishing laterality, for it is here that he discovers the one true constant in his universe. By experimenting with the forces of gravity, he learns how to control his body in order to gain the vital knowledge of one side versus the other.

Conversely, one must always remember what laterality is not. It is not handedness or dominance, and it is not the naming of sides. These are end products whose veridicality lies in the knowledge, without thinking, of two sides — laterality.

Directionality is exactly what it implies. It is a projection into space of this internal awareness of sides. It is the result of the intricate connection between the eyes and their monitoring of the body in space as it moves in a myriad of ways. It is the labeling or structuring of the world into reasonable coordinates.

It is important to remember that these coordinates must be well established within the individual before they can be projected into space. Once the child projects outside himself through directionality, he establishes objective space. He has therefore projected the directions, from himself to space, of right-left, up-down, and fore-aft. This simple progression is easily stated as: self-self, self-object, object-object.

As professionals or parents interested in these implications, the readers will find it imperative to thoroughly acquaint themselves with the writings of N. C. Kephart, Arnold Gesell, Jean Piaget, and J. H. Flavell.[1]

ACTIVITIES

SO FEW of the children referred to those of us who are educational therapists are "free" children — free to play with the spontaneity of unaffected children. They are the ones who avoid physical contact and activities that demand a certain degree of stamina. They withdraw into the background as their lack of coordination and their general timidity become apparent. Remember that by the time they have reached us they have gone through years of failure and ineptness, and they no longer desire to play the role of "court jester." What should be a time of initial learning has become a wasteland. It is up to us to encourage these children through planned successes. We must help them to realize the abilities of their bodies through constructive, directed exercises and games.

Since we have mentioned balance as a primary area of concern in developing laterality, we shall begin by presenting numerous suggestions that are adaptable to group situations. We are primarily interested in developing an awareness of muscle groups — their opposition for control of one side or another. Thus, we should place the children in every conceivable position that demands balance: lying, sitting, kneeling, and standing — stationary and mobile. We are further interested in developing the abilities of relaxation and concentration in order to accomplish our goal of body awareness. A rigid child is not learning about himself or his environment.

Balance.

Log rolling.

To develop the child's ability to roll (like a log), have him lie in a blanket. Pull on one edge of it and roll him off. Also, have him roll down hills and over inclined places.

Reaching out.

Lying both on the stomach and on the back, the child reaches out for objects at various heights. He is not to roll from side to side. Have him do the same while he is sitting and kneeling.

---

[1] Arnold Gesell, *Infancy and Human Growth* (New York, N.Y.: Harper and Brothers, 1940); J. H. Flavell, *The Developmental Psychology of Jean Piaget* (Princeton, N.J.: D. Van Nostrand, 1965); Jean Piaget, *The Origins of Intelligence in Children* (New York, N.Y.: International Universities Press, 1952); Newell C. Kephart, *The Slow Learner in the Classroom* (Columbus, Ohio: Charles E. Merrill, 1960), and *Learning Disabilities: An Educational Adventure* (West Lafayette, Ind.: Kappa Delta Pi Press, 1967).

LATERALITY AND DIRECTIONALITY

"T" stools.

"T" stools are simple to make. (See Figure 1.) Vary the heights and widths of the boards used so that the balancing task becomes more complicated. In the beginning, let the child sit on the stool with his back against a wall and his feet placed firmly on the floor. Progress to a point where his arms are in motion. As a variation, his feet may be elevated, etc. Play various games or do exercises while balancing.

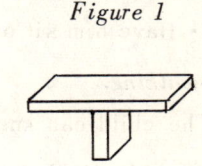

Figure 1

Balancing board.

As can be seen from the illustration in Figure 2, two variations of the balance board incorporates balance in two directions, then in four. Have the child balance on the board in sitting, kneeling, and standing positions.

Figure 2

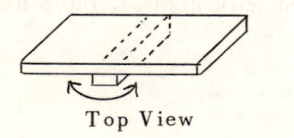

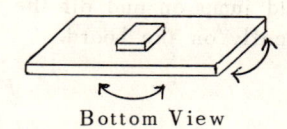

Top View   Bottom View

Innertubes.

Tractor-size innertubes may be used for exercises in the following ways:

• Have the child sit, kneel, and stand in and on the tubes. He may also straddle-bounce with them or creep or crawl around the edges and through a tire tunnel.

• The child can walk around a group of tubes using "ski poles" for support.

• Place side planks between the tubes and have the child traverse across them using a variety of body positions.

• Have the child walk with one foot on and the other foot off the tubes.

• Have him jump in and out of the tubes without touching the edges.

Barrels.

Barrels can be used for exercises in the following ways:

• Have the child straddle the barrel and rock from side to side. Have him lie on his stomach and do the same.

• Have him try various sitting and kneeling positions on the barrel while trying to keep his balance.

• Roll the barrel with the child inside while he is in a lying or sitting position.

Beach balls.

Have the child stoop and sit on a large beach ball or balloon. He may bounce it but must not break it.

SENSORY-MOTOR

Creeping.

Have the child balance while in a creeping position, extending various arm and leg combinations out from the body. The back must be kept level.

- Have the child creep up and down stairs, inclined planes, hills, etc.
- Have him sit on the stairway and bounce down.

Knee-walking.

The child can knee-walk on carpet-strip pathways, pillow courses, etc.

Kneeling blindfolded.

Blindfold the child and have him kneel on a square of carpet. Give him gentle pushes at various parts of his body and see if he can correct for balance by initiating movement of the body part only, not the entire body. Take note of his legs to see if they leave the ground. If they do so, they are tense.

Springboard.

The springboard is another device that can be made easily. (See Figure 3.) Have the child jump on and off the board with control. Have him jump up and down rhythmically on the board.

Figure 3

Walking on boxes.

A "walking box" is made for each of the child's feet. (See Figure 4.) The boxes must be sturdy enough to hold the child's weight and each one large enough to fit under one of his feet. A hole is drilled in each side of the box and a rope attached with which the child holds the box against his foot. The length of the rope will vary with the size of the child. The object is for the child to stand on the boxes, hold on to the rope, and walk in a coordinated manner.

Figure 4

Block obstacle course.

Design an obstacle course using blocks that are at least four inches in width. Begin by using two parallel rows of blocks, the left side for the left foot and the right side for the right foot. Increase the complexity of this design so that it resembles a Hop Scotch game. The child can vary the activity by touching the floor with his feet as he maneuvers over the course, or by keeping his feet on the blocks and not touching the floor with either foot. This can become very complicated by changing the spacing of the blocks as the child progresses through the course.

Space walk.

For the space walk, footprints are drawn on the ground. The child must place his feet on the prints and walk without losing his balance. Begin by drawing the footprints approximately one foot apart, gradually decrease the width to six inches, then to three inches. Finally, place the footprints so that one foot is placed directly in front of the other, with no space between.

Animal walks.

Have the child do various animal walks. For example:

• Bear walk: The child bends over from the waist and touches the floor with his hands, keeping his legs stiff. He moves forward, walking the hands and plodding the feet behind in a cross-lateral fashion. The head must be kept up.

• Ostrich walk: The child bends forward at the waist and grasps his ankles. See that his knees are as stiff as he can make them. He then walks forward, stretching his neck in and out.

• Frog walk: Have the child do a deep knee bend with hands on hips. He extends one leg to the side, then returns it. He then extends the other leg to the side and brings it back.

• Measuring worm: The child supports his body on his hands and toes. The arms are held straight, a shoulder width apart and directly under the shoulders. The body is kept in a straight line from head to toes. With the hands remaining stationary, the child walks his feet up to as close to his hands as possible, taking tiny steps. The body is not to sag. Next, keeping the feet stationary, he walks the hands forward in tiny steps until the first position is reached.

• Dog run: Have the child gallop by running forward with both hands on the floor and the knees slightly bent.

Races and relays.

The following games provide further variations in balancing activities.

• Balance race: Two lines, each consisting of three Indian clubs, are spaced about three feet apart. (Anything that stands about a foot and a half high, such as tall plastic bottles, may be used instead of Indian clubs.) From a line a few feet from the first clubs, two players start on signal and hop on both feet to the first club where they touch their foreheads to the top of the clubs, hop to the next club and repeat, etc. They may finish by hopping back over the same ground, touching each club with their foreheads, or they may hop directly back to the starting line. The winner is the one who finishes first without having lost his balance.

SENSORY-MOTOR

• Wheelbarrow race: A distance line should be marked fifty feet from the starting line. The players on each team pair off. The first player walks on his hands with his partner holding his ankles. After each pair has advanced in this fashion to the distance line, the players exchange positions and return to the starting line. After the first pair crosses the starting line, the next two players start.

• Dizzy Izzy race: At the signal to start, the first player in each line runs to the distance line where he picks up a bat. He stands one end of the bat on the ground and places his hand over the other end and the center of his forehead on the back of his hand. He circles around the bat five times, drops the bat, and walks rapidly to the starting line, where he takes his place at the back end of the line. This continues until each child has had a turn.

• Balance relay: The child walks erect, arms at sides, balancing an object on top of his head. If the object falls off, the player must stop, replace it, and then continue. He returns to the starting point and touches the second player, who then takes his turn.

Balance in place.

Designate a place where the child is to stand perfectly still and in balance. His heels must remain on the floor. Vary the distance between his feet.

Shoe boxes.

Place the child's feet in shoe boxes and have him walk a course such as is shown in Figure 5. (If preferred, extra large shoes or boots can be used instead of boxes.)

• Have the child place his feet in a confining box, then toss a ball at him. The child must duck to avoid the ball, yet maintain his balance.

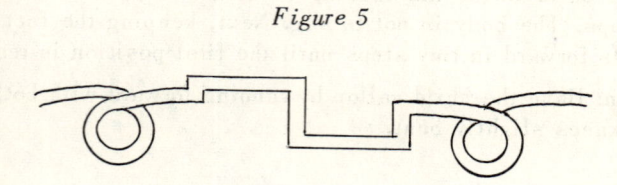

Figure 5

More exercises.

The following exercises suggest more positions for balance activities:

• Have the child balance on his seat, arms and legs up and extended. Vary the angle and position of the arms and legs. Have him hold a medicine ball in his hands or a basketball or bean bag between his legs.

• The child stands on his left foot, bends down, and supports his weight with his left hand. His right foot and hand are in the air. Have him decrease the distance between the supporting hand and leg. Have him place the supporting hand behind the supporting leg, first facing down and then facing up.

• The child balances on his head and one foot, then on one knee and one hand.

• Have the child stand, hands on hips, and rock fore and aft on his heels and toes.

Suggested props.

For balance exercises, one can adapt, in numerous ways, such items as ladders, dollys, balance boards, wagons, scooters, see-saws, and hammocks.

CHILDREN usually avoid laterality in one of two ways: They become entirely one-sided (completely unilateral) or they use both sides at the same time (completely bilateral). In either case, a thorough program of differentiation exercises should be incorporated into the child's physical-education program. This would include head, shoulder, trunk, arm, and leg differentiation exercises and, when appropriate, higher-level coordinated movements of the arm and leg. It would be impossible to offer suggestions here which would cover all of these areas. A brief outline of suggested activities will have to suffice.

Head exercises.

• Have the child do head lifts, drops, side-to-side rolls, rotations, etc., in all positions. He might also do simple and complex eye pursuit exercises, allowing his head to move with the moving target (a bouncing or rolling ball, a flashlight beam, moving objects, etc.).

• The child sits, stands, kneels, or lies in the prone position in front of a blackboard on which one-foot-square scribbles have been drawn. While the rest of his body is immobile, the child traces the scribbles with his nose, using head differentiation movements. His motions should be slow and controlled. He should not be permitted to become rigid.

Shoulder exercises.

• Have the child raise and lower his shoulders, move them forward and backward, and move them in rotation. This should be done first with both shoulders and then with one at a time.

Trunk exercises.

• The child sits, stands, or kneels as you toss a large beach ball toward him. Tell him in which direction he may bend (to the right or left, "toward the door," or "toward the window"). He should not be permitted to move his feet from one spot.

• Have the child lie on the floor in the supine position. Stand over him with one leg on either side of his hips. Drop a large ball to the right or left of his torso. He should sway his body by bending at the waist in order to avoid being hit by the ball. It will be necessary for him to keep his eyes on the ball at all times to avoid being hit when it drops.

SENSORY-MOTOR

• Have the child perform the following series: somersault, roll, somersault, roll. He should somersault head over heels, then roll his body over sideways. The sequence may be reversed so that he performs a backward somersault and a roll in the opposite direction. His performance should be rhythmical and smooth, with controlled movement. Have him work at first in a level area, then later, up and down an incline.

Bilateral arm and leg exercises.

• Have the child execute swings, sways, lifts, drops, and rotations of his arms and legs, as well as forward and backward movements.

• Modified isometric exercises may be introduced.

• Have the child do modified push-ups and chin-ups.

• Have him roll a ball, using even thrusts.

• Have him do prone and supine pushes and pulls.

• Attach three- or five-pound weights to two ropes which are swung over pulleys. The child will work the other ends of these ropes by pulling them with his head, hands, or feet during differentiation exercises. For example, he may sit on the floor and hold the ropes in either hand. As he raises or lowers his arms in a bilateral fashion, he is able to observe the movement of the weights. He will be able to see whether or not they are moving in a synchronized manner. You may place a yardstick or similar measuring device on the wall for pacing the activity. For example, ask the child to lower both of his arms simultaneously and observe the weights as they rise along the yardstick, etc. The same exercise may be done by manipulating the ropes and the weights with the legs, head, or trunk.

Coordination exercises.

• Have the child practice starting and stopping on command. This can be done while he is doing a variety of movements — running, jumping, hopping, gross motor movements, etc. Have him perform the activities while he is blindfolded so that he relies entirely on an auditory clue. Most of these exercises involve some kind of balancing activity because the child must learn to stop precisely at the time when he hears the signal.

• Following is a group of activities that the child can perform while he is sitting up so that he can watch both his arms and his legs move:

— The child puts his arms apart and together while a similar movement is being performed with the legs. In other words, he can feel what his arms are doing and see what his legs are doing, or vice versa. Have him use first one arm and one leg on the same side, then the other arm and leg on the other side; next, have him use both arms and legs.

— It might be beneficial to place a piece of light cord around the child's ankles and around his wrists so that when he lifts his hand he automatically lifts his legs at the same time. He can perform movements up and down, in and out, to the left and to the right, etc.

LATERALITY AND DIRECTIONALITY

— If possible, improvise a device that will make a sound, such as a bell sound, whenever the child reaches a full extension or a full closure. In this way he will be able to hear the simultaneity of his movements. I should imagine that a bell similar to the kind a teacher keeps on her desk could be used — when the little silver extending piece is touched, the bell sounds. This can also be done while the child is facing a mirror and standing against a wall; thus he is able to monitor his movements and correct his mistakes.

— Develop a wide variety of rhythmic movements using various arm and leg combinations.

— Have the child watch you as you do a rhythmic movement or perform a rhythmic sequence. Begin by using both hands and then have the child join in, perhaps with both his legs; or have him join in on the rhythm, making his head or his arms do the same movement, etc.

— Have the child perform all types of movements to a marching record or to some other record which he particularly enjoys.

Variations.

THE FOREGOING suggestions are valuable only to the extent to which they are varied. No one of these exercises should be repeated in exactly the same manner — some details should be changed to make the learning situation more meaningful. The following suggestions should be of assistance in teaching generalizations.

Changing positions.

Have the child change positions while lying on his back or stomach, kneeling, in a creeping stance, sitting (legs out straight, Indian style, leaning back on the knees, etc.), standing (with or without support, legs together or wide apart, in front of and behind the body, etc.), assuming pretzel shapes (entwining arms and legs), etc.

Further changes.

Have the child change the positions of his arms, legs, or head.

Pacing movements.

Have the child pace his movements to your count or words, to his own, to a rhythmic device such as a metronome, to your touch, to your movements (he watches you and moves with you), to a musical instrument, or to a simple marching record.

• Vary the speed of the rhythm — slow, moderate, fast. As the child progresses in doing an exercise, change the speed. If he loses control, have him stop immediately and regain control before continuing.

• Combine the ways in which you pace. For example: one-two, one-two, clap-clap, touch-touch, etc.

SENSORY-MOTOR

• Change the surface on which the child is performing: tile or wood floor, carpeting, earth and grass, a mattress, sand, in water, etc. Work on smooth, coarse, uneven, or hilly surfaces.

• Have the child do the exercises with and without a blindfold so that what he learns through a visual avenue he will also learn through a tactual avenue. It is necessary that all of his avenues work together so that the information he receives through one, he also receives through the other in a similar yet different manner. Remember that the child is so visually oriented that once the eyes are removed he becomes "on guard."

• When you are having the child perform these various activities and execute obstacle courses, use items salvaged from a variety of places, including your household or garage. Use ladders, boards, sheets of plywood, barrels, innertubes of all sizes, tires, boxes and cartons, ropes, pipe, jungle-gym equipment, blocks, sandboxes, sacks stuffed with different materials to give different feelings of pliability, cushions, chairs, tables, hose, rugs, brooms, buckets, etc. Make the courses real problem-solving situations so that the child has to think and perform in a flexible way. Vary by having him carry something while going through the course — or have him strap a knapsack on his back.

• Add distracting stimuli, but do so gradually. In other words, can the child, after he seems to know how to move in a particularly paced way, still keep moving rhythmically if you start clapping or talking or if you turn on soft music?

• Add delays. After you have told, shown, and manipulated the child through a sequence, wait a few moments, not allowing him to verbalize the sequence you have just asked for.

• Sequence the movements or tasks.

• Allow the child to feel you as you make the movements. Do the movements while you are relaxed and then while you are tense so that he can feel or see the right and wrong ways.

• Vary the amount and type of clothing worn by the child. Complicate the task by using articles that are too large or too bulky for him.

• Weight down different limbs so that the child becomes aware of the side or sides that are not being used properly. Place equal weights on both limbs, or increase the weight on one side and not the other.

THE EMPHASIS of this paper has been on motor skills. This is necessarily so, because one will never be able to "teach" laterality — the child must experience it in the essence, and thereby fully understand himself. The appropriate language concepts will be readily mastered once the foundations are provided. For years we have been trying unsuccessfully to begin with academics to find an answer. In so doing, we have provided the child with numerous crutches and have assisted him in organizing his letters, numbers, paper, etc., in an inconsistent manner. In other words, sometimes he seems to retain his "laterality"; most often he is in a state of hesitation and confusion.

Where does the answer lie? Perhaps we'll never really know. From the evidence of recent research and teaching practices, however, we are certainly able to surmise that the importance of perceptual-motor training has all too long been underrated or forgotten. In reality, one has but to study the first few years of a child's life in order to understand the unequivocal relationship between movement experience and readiness for continued learning.

The importance of a total space concept prior to reading, writing, arithmetic, and spelling can be understood easily by every person. Just spend a moment envisioning your world and all the aforementioned means of communication without the benefit of *right-left, up-down, top-bottom,* and *beside* relationships. You would be totally confused and lost in an alien environment. If the understanding of basic language concepts is absent, then all other types of sequential expressions are meaningless, for wherein lies one's point of reference? You have seen this child, for he leaves his mark at every turn . . .

. . . and his words on all our lips: "I didn't understand . . . " — "But that's a *b*. . . ." — "I'll show you. . . . Look . . . oh . . . I thought . . . " — "Please help me! . . . Am I retarded?"

As professionals, it is our responsibility to help this child find himself in his own space world so that he can move on to solidly based growth in the area of academics, as well as in his personal and social development.

REFERENCES

Chaney, Clara, *Motoric Aids to Perceptual Training.* Columbus, Ohio: Charles E. Merrill, 1968.

Cruickshank, William M., and others. *A Teaching Method for Brain-Injured and Hyperactive Children.* Syracuse, N.Y.: Syracuse, University Press, 1961.

Ebersole, Marylou, Newell C. Kephart, and James B. Ebersole. *Steps to Achievement for the Slow Learner.* Columbus, Ohio: Charles E. Merrill, 1968.

Hackett, Layne C., and Robert G. Jensen. *A Guide to Movement Exploration.* Palo Alto, Calif.: Peek Publishing Co., 1967.

Mosston, Muska. *Developmental Movement.* Columbus, Ohio: Charles E. Merrill, 1965.

Petitclerc, Grace M. "Relaxation and Concentration," *Teaching Educationally Handicapped Children.* Edited by John I. Arena. San Rafael, Calif.: Academic Therapy Publications, 1967.

Spalding, Romaldo Bishop, and Walter T. Spalding. *The Writing Road to Reading.* New York, N.Y.: William Morrow, 1962.

SENSORY-MOTOR

MATERIALS

There are many commercial materials available that can be utilized in helping children to improve abilities that have not developed properly because of neurological deficits. Following are a few of the sources for materials that have been found particularly helpful.

Sullivan Programmed Reading (1965) and a kit of materials (Getman program), *Developing Learning Readiness* (1968), are available from McGraw-Hill Book Company, Webster Division. Also available from McGraw-Hill is *Kindergarten Evaluation of Learning Potential* (1967).

Pictures and Patterns (Frostig program) may be obtained from Follett Publishing Company, Chicago, Illinois (1964), and the *Parkinson Program for Special Children* (1968) may be obtained from that company's Parkinson Division in Champaign, Illinois.

Mathematics with Numbers in Color is available from the Cuisenaire Company of America (1966), and the Dubnoff program, the Erie program, and the Fairbanks-Robinson program are available from Teaching Resources, Boston, Massachusetts (1967).

Other companies that have helpful materials available are Continental Press, Elizabethtown, Pennsylvania; Educational Development Laboratories (a division of McGraw-Hill), Huntington, New York; and Science Research Associates Reading Laboratories, Chicago, Illinois.

Body Image and Body Awareness

Grace Petitclerc

BODY IMAGE is most clearly defined as that which we hold to be true about our physical make-up and the way it functions. A concept or impression is formed about the body by experiences — good or bad, successes or failures — which occur from the cradle to the present and which are vivid enough to make an imprint in the areas of memory. From there, our thinking and acting are conditioned.

Once a belief concerning the body and its operation, whether reality or illusion, is securely imbedded in this picture, our character and behavior are colored from that aspect of certainty. This image, however, can be changed. It takes effort, concentration, self-reeducation, but it can be changed.

Body awareness, on the other hand, defined in the light of today's isotronic analysis, reaches into a new dimension of physiomental growth.[1] Here, we learn of mounting and expanding relationships between the self and the not-self, between the animate and the inanimate, the concrete and the abstract, the functional and the creative — an area where change, action, and communication now are almost instantaneous. To enter such areas of awareness and perform successfully, the body image must be full-grown and wholly integrated so that every purpose and possibility within the individual may be brought into flower.

Body awareness is a constantly changing, expanding growth that is pushing the limits of achievement and discovery farther and farther beyond the horizon of existing probabilities.

Building the body image.

Body image is built by our own conception of ourselves, brought about from the first sensory stimulation in the cradle through every experience during our growing up until the composite picture is complete, wholesome, and satisfying. Should it fall short of wholesome completion, the individual remains caught up somewhere in the initial stages of personal development, unable to advance into his environment and to accept a profitable and satisfying life.

---

[1] Isotronics is defined as a system of inner exploration; a controlled process of sensory examination; cybernetics.

In this context, it is said of children, with whom we are here concerned: "One of the tenets in teaching the so-called normal child is that he will not learn until a certain stage of maturation has been achieved. It is also an accepted fact that different aspects of the child mature at different rates."[2] If these are accepted facts for the so-called normal child, how much more are they facts for the inconsistently functioning child?

He who fails to mature.

All school curricula is based on the assumption that each child entering school for the first time has achieved that stage of maturity where he is physically able, emotionally free, and neurologically coordinated for learning. And what stigmas fall upon either the normal child or the inconsistently functioning child who fails to perform at this level?

It is imperative, therefore, that all children are assisted to physical, emotional, and neurological maturity by a consistent body-image development program. To further emphasize the importance of such a consideration, it has been proven in a number of recent studies that the intellectual development of children who lack responsive vehicles for input and output is stunted — the natural intelligence gives up in frustration.[3]

The first step.

A BODY-IMAGE developmental program must start at the beginning with the first sensory impulses that generate a body image. This may seem to some to be a bit of wagwit; however, from the standpoint of logic, if we bypass even a small detail in the first learning patterns, we may invite a big problem further on.

In addition, no diagnosis yet devised has been able to measure the exact experience loss in the human organism's learning patterns or to pinpoint when or where the loss occurred, no matter how comprehensive the medical, psychological, or educational examination may be. The missing experience lies hidden in some indeterminate memory area, enmeshed in obscure timing and circumstances.

Therefore, we have no choice but to commence at the beginning and to continue through the whole process of body-image building in as detailed and as thorough a program as is possible.

The primitive beginning.

The first sensory reaction in infancy begins with the stimulation received from different textured materials that rub on the skin. Subsequently, for a deeper-than-skin sensitizing, the hands smooth, pinch, pat, slap, squeeze, and pound. Soon, a consciousness of body length develops as the feet push against the bottom of the crib and the hands reach above the head. Next, many awarenesses

---

[2]Ruth Millburn Clark, "Psychological Aspects of Speech and Hearing," in *The Characteristics of Infantile Thinking and Body Image*, Part III (Springfield, Ill.: Charles C. Thomas, 1960).

[3]Joseph McVicker Hunt, *Intelligence and Experience* (New York, N.Y.: Ronald Press, 1961).

develop: muscles stretching in the extremities and in the torso; the sensation of water moving over the body; the feel of talcum powder and ointments; the soothing touch of cotton and the harsh contact of cloth on raw buttocks; and finally, the the response to muscle and nerve working together — crawling, scooting, or rolling over various textures.

Comingled with each of these experiences is a growing cognizance of the sounds that accompany each tactile-sensory response. Here, too, the frequency of each stimulation begins establishing a rhythm concomitant or counter-concomitant with certain rhythmic actions inside the body; in either case, the effect of nerve stimulation toward maturation is compounded.

What is "moving toward maturity"?

Growth toward maturity is described as the "cephalocaudal flow" — from head to tail growth.[4] During this growth period, eye-hand coordinations, nerve-muscle affinity, and memory commence. Here, also, eye-muscle control begins, and the seed of visual perception becomes implanted in productive tissues. A significant development is the foundation for translating sound perception into symbolic meaning.

On this first translation of a sensory impulse into meaning rests all the future multiple translations from other sensory impulses that will take place for a lifetime of coordinated learning and action. Whichever sense that takes a headstart toward maturity sets the pattern that undergirds maturity in all the others.

Simulating a primitive learning.

Primitive experiences can be simulated for the older child as exercises on the horizontal that are fun — without reference to the cradle, of course. Children like to use the word "dimension," so this could be described as the first-dimension exploration.

Have the child dress in swim trunks, rub his body with sand, then have him take a cool shower. A rubdown with salt before a shower or a dip in a pool gives a deeper stimulation. This being impossible in a classroom, use sandpaper followed by cotton on all exposed skin areas. If these exercises are performed in a group, have two or three children at a time lie on the floor while experiencing them. If they are performed in a one-to-one teaching situation, both the teacher and the child should lie on the floor.

After the first introductory experience, in which the friction on the body and the contrast in stimulation creates sound through the organism, translate the body learning into verbal recognition; talk about everything that is done, as it is done, and talk about how it feels. Ask the child if he likes it or not? Do each exercise at least three times, and on the third time, in addition to verbalization, translate the experience onto a piece of paper with colored chalk. Any kind of line or form that expresses the experience is acceptable.

---

[4] Paul A. Lewis, "Implications for the Development of Visual Function," *Exceptional Children* (April 11, 1959).

SENSORY-MOTOR

Be prepared to invent ways and means and innovative applications for stimulating the tactile sense and for bringing the action into recognition with each growth need on the horizontal. To what has been suggested as necessary in this dimension, an inventive teacher can add and adapt means of translating the experience more effectively to the class — or to the individual — than can be done by following specific examples.

The upper half of the first dimension.

ADVANCING to maturity of coordinated effort within the first premises of growth, the human crawls, scoots, stretches in all directions, rolls, and swims — on the floor or in water. Competitive games can be made out of these activities by having the child compete with himself.

"See how long it takes you to roll from this point to that one. I'll time you."

The child rolls.

"Fine. Now try it again and see if you can better your time."

He rolls again.

"Excellent. You cut off three seconds. Let's see if you can cut off five seconds this time."

In reeducation, motivation is the key that turns the dial from boredom to learning. Repetition is absolutely necessary, and much repetition can be squeezed out of an exercise. Adding the rhythm of time — for fun, not for pressure — is one of the few elements of motivation possible on the horizontal. While the child lies on the floor or couch, training in listening to develop sound memory and discrimination can be fun in itself. It is easier to invent motivation in listening.

"Listen to this tone and tell me when you can no longer hear it inside or outside your head." . . . "Could you hear it inside?" . . . "Try this tone and see if you can hear it longer." . . . "What is the difference between this tone and the first one?" . . . "Listen to the two tones with the beat of one, two, three." . . . "Which had one beat and which had two beats?" . . . "Now, turn over on your stomach and let me pound your back while you make a loud noise in your throat. See if you can hear that noise way down into your toes."

After the child has listened for a time to the loud noise going through his body, call attention to the rhythm it makes. "If your body were a drum, what kind of a beat would you be making? Count it off by yourself."[5]

Growth never advances singly, to the exclusion of development in other parts of the organism; so, while the areas of feeling and sound seem to have leapt ahead, the rest of the family of senses is actually being nourished by their leaders' acceleration. Because of this deep sense of cooperation, we include the less-active senses in this horizontal practice.

---

[5] Christian Volf, *Acoustic Reflex Theory* (Ober Osterich, Austria: Gallspach, 1949); reprinted in the *Journal of the Scientific Association for Ultrasonic Research* (September 1957); reprinted in English (Monterey, Calif.: D'Angelo Publications, 1964). See also, Georgia T. Cooper, *Exploring Immaturity in Capable Children* (Pleasant Hill, Calif.: Contra Costa County Department of Education, 1964).

All sense experience while lying supine is oddly different from that experienced in any other position. Therefore, to increase stimulation with taste and smell when practicing sense experience with older children, we ask questions to draw in the mental aspect of comparison. To illustrate: "Does this taste as sour as you remember it when you tasted it sitting up?" . . . "If you were eating this while sitting at a table, do you think it would taste the same or different? How different?" . . . "What does this smell make you think of? Did you smell the fragrance you just named while you were lying down or standing up?"

With sight, however, we present an object swinging above the face — an object that also has sound to lead vision into action. The sound may be pleasant or unpleasant. The object is swung forward and backward, side to side, around and around, and we merely say, "Watch it."[6]

Step into the vertical.

FROM the horizontal we proceed into the vertical. At this level, the human organism learns to sit upright, stand upright, jump up or down, stretch up or down, reach and grasp and lean with the weight of the body on the feet, seat, or hands, and many intricate vertical acts related to this posture.

Balance is achieved in the vertical dimension. Fluid equilibrium and a conscious relationship with rhythm is basic to number concept — a concept implanted in the metabolic action of the whole organism which, to be fulfilled, must consummate in outer expression.[7] Taste and smell take on a new prominence from this upright position, and the eyes are beginning to see — not merely to follow — an object moving in front of the face. Responses to hot and cold, pleasure and displeasure, endearment or rejection are actively evident.

Meanwhile, everything learned on the horizontal is being absorbed and digested with each new feature developed at this level of growth. Total assimilation takes over.

Spoof or proof?

Such statements as the above would be a mere guess — a far-fetched one — were it not for such pioneer investigations as those conducted at McGill and Princeton universities from 1951 to 1962. These studies tried to determine what learned patterns remained when the present stimuli were rolled back to the horizontal. They were called "experiments in sensory deprivation."[8]

A university student, who possessed full awareness and whose faculties were intact, was incarcerated for four days in a closed cell without light, sound,

---

[6] G. N. Getman, "The Visuomotor Complex in the Acquisition of Learning Skills," *Learning Disorders, Volume I*, ed. Jerome Hellmuth (Seattle, Wash.: Special Child Publications, 1965).

[7] John F. Gardner, *The Experience of Knowledge* (Garden City, N.Y.: Myrin Institute, 1962).

[8] E. G. Boring, *Sensation and Perception in the History of Experimental Psychology* (New York, N.Y.: Appleton-Century, 1960).

or other stimuli of any kind. He lay on a cot without moving except when necessary. At the end of the trial, he was removed and tested. All sense of possessing a body had gone. His muscular control, coordinations, and balance were unmanageable. Sound perception and visual perception were shattered. Objects in the test room appeared to him as flat extensions of himself. Some memory of words and sounds remained, but their meaning escaped him. He could neither read nor write.

All that remained intact was an ability to stretch lying down and an inner consciousness that his mental commands were not getting through to his exterior. This condition, of course, lasted only a short time.

These findings are, it seems to me, of tremendous value to those of us who work with inconsistently functioning children.

Deeper understanding.

When we see a baby being bounced up and down on its mother's knee in a rhythmic pattern do we understand, in a broader meaning, what growth is taking place? Could it be the same growth as an older child is experiencing while bouncing on a trampoline? Is a baby tottering across the floor unaided finding the same balance as a small girl, face shining, tottering along on a balance board by herself? When we watch a small child grasp an object in front of its face, pull it down to its body, then up to its mouth, do we recognize the basic value in some of the eye-training exercises?

Stimulating the second level.

MOST of the second-dimension growth patterns are simulated and practiced in comprehensive physical-education programs: leaping, jumping, tumbling, head stands, hand walking, bar work, swimming, trampoline, weight lifting, shot put, target games, climbing, balancing, judo, walking — with or without something to balance on the head — obstacle games, hula hoops, stilts, and all manner of rhythmic body movements to one's own rhythm or to an imposed rhythm.[9] It is necessary that every child be a skilled performer in all these exercises. Before the child is presented with the next level of growth, the exercises must be repeated, until the muscle-nerve patterns respond without deviation.

An additional help to older children in establishing the skills is to verbalize about the action in the exerxise. Sound and action together implant the process in memory. Also, state which side of the body is being used as it moves — right or left, front or back. The fixing of correct laterality can be rooted here.

As shall be shown, all patterns perfected at this stage of development shoulder the burden of the initial acquisition of academic skills. Children still growing on the second level take out of the physical skills mentioned above only the most elemental performances. For this reason, physical-education teachers should never press for sophisticated perfection from these children. At the next stage — as part of natural growth — physical skills will take on new breadth and depth

---

[9] Layne C. Hackett and Robert Jenson, *A Guide to Movement Exploration* (Palo Alto, Calif.: Peek Publishers, 1966).

into which the original simple patterns will be absorbed. After this expansion is achieved and fixed, the child must reach back and recap his original second-dimension facilities to find a basis for academic expertness. This is difficult for most. It is impossible for a few, unless they receive help from a teacher with the necessary insight.

The third dimension.

At the third level of development, I am reminded of the axiom: "Different aspects of the child mature at different rates." Allowances must be made in our measuring and testing, in academic scheduling, and in grade placements for the divine prerogative given every human — to mature in his own design and to take as long as he needs to do it.

Children know when some facet is missing in their makeup and when they are not ready to accept certain challenges. An unconscious something tells them to take a little longer to practice and to gain confident support for strength to go on.

I once had a six-year-old boy in school who was uncertain of himself in new relationships. He had experienced confident success at his own little table where his name was posted and his books and personal treasures were secure. Whenever he failed, or was in danger of failing, he would run back to his haven, sit down for a moment, then advance once more into the arena of action that had challenged his confidence. At last the day came when he no longer needed this sort of strengthening. He had learned to meet new confrontations head-on.

What if he had not been allowed to run from the group to recharge himself? If he had been reprimanded or shamed or penalized, his fragmented self-image would have needed to be rebuilt at some later date, or it would have limited him for all of his days.

These potholes in our growing do not erase themselves. They are only brought into level adjustment by concentrated effort, patience, and gentle understanding.

Depth perception.

AT THIS THIRD stage, all the senses focus into depth perception. In this dimension, they integrate into a single unit, comparable to a well-organized business unit, each department serving a supportive role to the whole. The visual department is the last to slip into place, and it then proceeds to outstrip all the others in breadth of capacity.[10]

Sound perception at this level advances into conscious hearing with the apparatus; it appropriates the whole body torso and its cavities as a sounding board that serves as a tremendous synthesizer for all the family of senses as they grow toward maturation. Therefore, if we have left a pothole in the child's

---

[10] Ira J. Gordon, *Human Development* (New York, N.Y.: Harper Brothers, 1962); Michael S. Gazzaniga, R. W. Sperry, P. H. Vogel, and J. E. Bogen, "The Split Brain in Man," *The Scientific American* (August 1967).

sound reception, it could cause delay in maturation for all the other senses as well.[11]

Sight moves toward maturity.

Prematurely, at this point, we begin to expect an almost underachievable performance from sight: complex eye-muscle control from still undeveloped muscles (muscles to control eye focus) that are new to their job; instantaneous eye-focus adjustment (near point and far point) from muscle-nerve-tissue-mind coordination that has never coordinated before; and eye perception in time and space relationships that requires a completely new pattern of operation and inner communication that should be allowed years to mature. Investigations in this field disclose that the eye is not mature until the individual reaches twelve years.[12]

If we understood what we were asking, we might be ashamed and revise our expectations — that is, if our shame were large enough and deep enough to overshadow our immense egocentric ambition to exploit our children. If a child is able to learn to read at the age of four or five, this is often accomplished at the expense of the future health of his eyes.

Of course, learning by experience — recognizing and perceiving objects and their relationships in depth — is necessary at this stage, and it is natural.[13] It is essential to the progression of eye maturity, for children to feel and listen, look and name all kinds of forms in all kinds of situations where length, height, and depth are concerned, as well as to broaden consciousness and build vocabulary-learning skills that require seeing to perfect. But when we expect eye focus on minute differences of form — particularly when the form is a two-dimensional representation of black and white pictures or symbols (letters and numbers) which entail another learning process for interpretation — we are asking for large trouble — and I think we have it.

Some children learn to read those flat symbols on their own at an early age. This is their educational prerogative, as well as their physiogenetic prerogative. We have no right to interfere with these prerogatives, and we have no jurisdiction over them. However, if we gave all children their right to learn on their own whenever they were mature enough, whenever their body images were complete — whether they were six or sixteen — we would have no reading problems. I have had children who were nine and ten — and several who were twelve — who had never read before and who just picked up a book and started to read. All at once they were ready, and all of their sensory tools were trained and integrated.

---

[11]Peter F. Ostwald, "Human Sounds," in *Psychological and Psychiatric Aspects of Speech and Hearing*, Part I (Springfield, Ill.: Charles C. Thomas, 1969).

[12]Paul A. Lewis, *op. cit.*

[13]G. N. Getman, *op. cit.*

Experience in the third dimension.

LEARNING about depth is exhilarating whether we look at it with young children or with older ones who are picking up missing areas in their sensory tools. Here, the human organism is being delivered from physical confinement and limitations for the third time, and the whole child lets loose.

Every action is volatile and extreme. The child shouts, screams and laughs, sings and swears at the top of his lungs. He fights for the fun of contact, he runs at high speed everywhere; he slams doors, kicks over chairs, and breaks windows. Objects flying through space — broken glass or blocks or balls — are essential to his growing consciousness of space.

He must experience and reexperience his delivery, too. He needs to enclose himself in a small, tight place — under a bed, in a barrel or a box, in a playhouse, under a sheet — and burst out with a great shout of joy. Mothers and teachers often disapprove of this sort of play, especially if something is broken or torn (as often happens), but if they only realized what this exercise did for the child they would see that nothing could be as important for him as having this experience.

Experience in the third dimension must always be a total experience. The senses are now ready to learn how to act as a unit and the materials and opportunities we give children should provide for this total stimulation — tactile, hearing, taste (if nothing more than saliva gathering in the mouth due to excitement), smell, and sight.[14] Yet, a child sitting in a classroom is asked to use only sight.

To complete the body image.

It is time for the body to become a tangible reality in the mind's eye of the child, recognized by all his senses and accepted as an effective, worthy vehicle. It seems that after all the inner sensory channels are functioning as a unit it is necessary to obtain a conscious approval and a convincing appraisal of the outer covering. It seals the unit as topnotch and complete for service.

Have the child stand in front of a full-length mirror. You stand with him to avoid the destructive force of self-consciousness entering. First you admire your eyes, then explore with your hands to add tactile sensation and sound, awareness and function. At some point during the exploration, eat and smell something, noting muscular movements, facial expressions, and any other sensations.

Here is the opportunity to tap on the door of emotional stability. Here, the child can begin consciously liking himself for the way he looks, feels, and operates. He can begin judging the things of which he is capable and the things which he still needs to develop. He can begin to evaluate himself without shame or self-condemnation, understanding how the human grows.

"I like my hair. I like the color of it and the feel of it." . . . "What good does it do for me? How does it grow on my head? Where does it come from?" . . .

---

[14]Kuniyoshi Obara, *Education of the Whole Man* (Machida City, Tokyo, Japan: Tamagawa University Press, 1960).

"So, that is the shape of my head! What is it called? What is inside? Yes, I think it is a good brain. How does it work?" . . . "I like the color of my eyes. I think they are shaped like two marbles. Tell me how they work for me."

A badge of graduation.

THE ENTIRE outer design of the body is felt, compared, inquired into and praised for its service to the being who occupies the three-dimensional form. Repeat this exploration as often as possible, with any sort of motivation possible, until an attempt can be made to sculpt a human likeness in clay.

By sculpting a man in clay, the child makes only one transfer or translation of what he has learned: from the human size to the clay model size. His ability to build and represent in three dimensions has already been developed into skills — building a bird house or playhouse, carving in wood or soap, other clay modeling of animals and various forms, and any number of crafts, arts, and sciences.

On the other hand, the Draw-a-Man technique requires three translations all at once: from human size to paper size, from three dimensional to two dimensional, and from the open-hand feel of the form to the closed manipulation with a pencil.[15]

The likeness in clay does not need to look like the one who sculpts it — though it may well do so. It need only follow the basic design of human outer appearance. It always proves to be a badge of graduation for the child. Several children have told me that as they carried the figure home they felt inside themselves that they had grown up and could take care of themselves, and could now face whatever they had to meet.

If the child wants to fire his figure to preserve it, the clay figure must be cut open and the insides cut out. One little girl was most anxious to preserve her figure, but she would not cut it open and dig the insides out. She did not want to lose the brains she had found out that she had.[16] This sort of identification is always present with this exercise.

Body image and academic achievement.

I know of two school systems which begin each school year with a body-image developmental program for all grades. The upper grades also are introduced to an awareness routine. This practice is said to pay off with a marked increase in academic achievement. Why not try it?

In the classroom, the procedure should follow a sequence comparable to that growth sequence found in each stage of human development. Use your own ingenuity and as much latitude as your principals will allow in adapting the horizontal activities to your children's needs. While lying on the floor, listen to drums, sounds, simple music, or a story. Let the children crawl through a barrel or a long cardboard tube. Learn to use rulers, compasses, calipers, and protractors on the floor. Create designs with odd discards. Conduct feeling experiences; especially,

---

[15] Florence Goodenough, *Measurement of Intelligence* (Yonkers, N.Y.: World Book, 1926).

[16] John Holt, *How Children Learn* (New York, N.Y.: Pitman, 1967).

let the children feel letters made of plastic or cut from wood, without saying what they are.

When the children have become apathetic about finger painting, introduce organized group finger painting and make large loops, circles, and straight lines — teacher and children together — in rhythm. Verbalize: "Loop, loop, loop; circle, circle, circle; straight, straight, straight; up-down, up-down, up-down; dot, dot, dot." . . . "We stop and start over when we get to the dot." . . . "Listen — dot — stop. Is there anything in there that sounds the same?" Repeat this exercise many times for fun.

Writing — the beginning of academics.

ONE DAY, the teacher lifts her painting off the floor onto a table, letting the children follow at their own will. (Activities on the floor are supportive, community things, so let children enjoy that feeling of interrelationship until they are ready to feel separative and individualistic at their own table, in an upright position.)

From this new position, the teacher leads the children into writing a word, just for fun: loop, circle, up-down, up, circle, dot. When success is achieved, after many repetitions, and all of the children are standing at their tables, the teacher adds the lifting of the tongue with the loop, the rounding of the lips with the circle, a breath taken in and a puff with the up-down, up, circle, and a click of the tongue for the dot. It takes care and a great deal of ingenuity to maintain the fun in this association while at the same time working to achieve success.

It is important to recognize the levels of memory being stirred to fortify and make meaningful and successful the complex learning expected of children who are in school at an age when their body image can only be on the threshold of maturity.[17]

Next, associate the sound with the action developed from the tongue and mouth positions: the loop, circle, up-down, up, circle, dot. The teacher makes the loop on the board and puts her finger on the base of the loop. "Make a loop and put your finger the way mine is. Now, go over the loop with your finger, lift your tongue at the same time, and make a noise in your throat. What do you hear?"

The children's eyes focus to near point, to far, to near. They compare their loop with the loop made by the teacher; then their ears listen near and far at the same time — if they are able — to compare the noise that they make with the noise that their teacher makes. These steps accomplished, they advance to the other forms with their sounds: *l-a-p;* then, for fun, they turn the letters end-to-beginning and hear the sounds with the letters arranged in this way: *p-a-l.* By this time, saying the sounds quickly, the two words appear in mind, ear, body.

---

[17] Louise S. Sinderson, "Teaching the Brain-Injured Child," *Journal for Exceptional Children* (April 1960).

SENSORY-MOTOR

Spelling and reading come into focus.

Allow the children to act out each word as it appears in their minds — first as if they were forming the letters with their bodies on a trampoline or the tumbling mat, then for word meaning and association. Let them choose words from the experience stories written each morning with the teacher on their large experience charts for continued fun in writing and continued skill in forming letters. Graduate from finger paints to dry calcium paint with fingers on rough paper, to wet paint with brushes, to colored pencils, and finally to lead pencils and white paper.

Without the children realizing it, a spelling list evolves out of their own usage. Could this be the corroborant to reanimate spelling, the weakest skill in the curricula of our schools?

Follow up by translating spelling into reading. Copy the group stories on a bulletin-type typewriter and have the children sew the pages into books so that each child can have his own. Practice reading the books all together, fingers on the line for eye training, turning the pages together for training in eye movement from the right bottom of the page to the top left, and the teacher leading out with colorful inflections and a quality of adventure in her voice. When you come to one of the spelling words, stop and let one — or a dozen — of the children call out the word. They will be so excited that they will scarcely be able to wait for the next reading time.

Meanwhile, reactivate the activity of feeling the plastic or wooden letters, now taking note of their resemblances to and differences from the letters the children write, and learning the names of the letters. Let the children form their spelling words with the loose letters and begin making up sentences. If it is possible to have a typewriter in the room, let the children transfer their word knowledge onto the machine. Let the group choose one of its members each morning to read the written experience story all the way through all by himself. Have the story copied on the typewriter and give a copy to each child. Let the children choose from among themselves a "teacher" who picks out a sentence from the story on the chart that each child finds on his page. The children gain confidence and skill in these activities — which are in familiar, confident territory — before advancing to books made by someone else and from a point of view that is outside of their own living context.

Soon, most of the children will be reading everything within their ability that they can find. Of course, the teacher remembers and gives understanding allowance to the few children whose body image takes longer to build.

Numbers and math.

NUMBER symbols require the same approach and development as letter symbols, and the same pitfalls account for the way they puzzle some children. When processes in calculation and problem solving are introduced, the child whose third-dimension perception is not yet fully oriented will have trouble. It is better to wait for the development of his body image.

Numerical computations are action itself — often quick, drastic action that leaps forward and backward, up and down — that grows and diminishes. A child who is expert in computations must be well coordinated, graceful, and facile in body movement — quick and alert in physical contacts. This testimony is the gift of both Germany and Japan. In world surveys, the people of these countries lead in arithmetical and mathematical expertness.

Mathematical concepts, on the other hand, are a product of the creative intuition and inventive genius of those whose body awareness has reached out and found answers.

Body awareness.

Cultivation of awareness — outward and inward, beyond that which can be seen with present sight or felt by and responded to by any of the other senses that coordinate information through body, brain, mind — has only recently come to be an adventure entered into openly. This adventure has been the private exploit of poets, musicians, artists, and others of their ilk — all a little mad, yet fascinating and sought after for the beauty they create. All at once, this situation has changed and the development of greater awareness is examined and explored on every hand.

Oddly enough, this dimension, which most of us who are adult are only beginning to explore, is familiar to the majority of our so-called inconsistently functioning children. Their unanchored position, in our special concept of reality, puts them in rapport with a world which is an extension of their own thinking, in empathy with things and actions as part and parcel of their own energies.[18] It is no farfetched supposition to them that they can develop a set of higher senses to see across the world or inside an atom, to feel things happen anywhere, to hear voices still lingering in the air though the speakers are gone or not yet born. These children — and McLuhan — can envision their faculties replacing the machines now in use.

Again, oddly enough, while some of us recognize these children as creative geniuses, we demand that they compress their higher faculties into the same mold which limits us. Our purpose is to have them experience as we are experiencing — logically and sanely — so that we can make sense out of their thoughts and actions. Probably this is right. No human entity should miss a level of growth; and some of our children are conceding to our demands. Others are not. But whether they are or not, we can advance into an understanding that gives purpose and validity in our eyes to whatever these children do and wherever they must go.

Rational training in nonrational areas.

THE FIRST STEP in body awareness is the stimulation and direction of the imagination. At this stage, no reason or logic should be asked for or expected as the imagination is released and allowed to function freely. With children whose imagination has not been awakened, I begin with a feeling exercise which produces the ability to visualize. That is, I help the children to make an image in the mind's eye or in the inner hearing — an ability necessary to refined, ecumenic

---

[18] Marshall McLuhan, *Understanding Media: The Extensions of Man* (New York, N.Y.: The New American Library Press, 1964).

SENSORY-MOTOR

reading or listening — then float the image on the emerging energies, as in a fanciful dream.

To illustrate: place three solid basic wooden forms — a pyramid, a cube, and a sphere — in front of the person entering the experiment. Ask him to close his eyes and take one form in both hands and feel it carefully. Now, have him open his eyes and look at the form. Again, have him close his eyes, feel the form, and develop an exact image of the form behind his eyes. If this cannot be done, have him repeat the look and feel and visualize the form until the image is clear and solid enough to stay while the form is manipulated. For some children, this takes lengthy practice.

Once the image is stable, have the child relate this form to parts of the body which are designed in the same shape. Verbalize these relationships. Then repeat the procedure using another of the wooden forms. After that, repeat the procedure with the last block. Now, have the child bring all three forms together in visual image, with any kind of background, without feeling or looking.

In his imagined design, have the child color each of the three forms a different color. Tell him to try to see the color penetrating the form so it is dyed all the way through. Then, tell him to see each form dividing into two forms, the same color, the same size. Tell him to let each divide again, slowly, so that the four forms of each form can be kept clearly in visual consciousness. Now, tell him to assemble the twelve forms in the likeness of a body, remembering the forms in his own body which can walk and move. Otherwise, the design is not required to be anything ever seen before.

Have the child let the body move freely — kick, throw, jump, wheel around, fall down — and let the movement be felt in his own muscles, bones, and flesh. Have him take it slowly, but he should feel it intensely.

Feeling and sound.

NOTE THAT exploration develops concentration, and concentration is required for abstract thinking and for creative mutation that is of use to humanity — the end product of awareness and expanded faculties. After the imagination is stimulated, the resulting energies released need to be cohered, like a laser beam, and brought into synergic purpose. The nature of that purpose rests with the integrity and dedication of each one who creates.

With every exploration, proceed more slowly, experience intensely. Prolong the concentration, thus gaining control and direction of very powerful instruments. Even in children's hands, these can be instruments for great good.

Sound adds a great new area into body awareness. Try it. Pat smartly all over the body, beginning at the center and going toward the sides and the ends of the extremities. Give the neck, face, and head a particularly vigorous patting. If any parts have stopped tingling by the time the whole body has been covered, go back and pat those parts again. The body must tingle all over as one tingling unit, with the sound of patting felt and heard throughout.

Let every inch of your body feel as if it were swelling with vibration. At a certain point, let the vibration begin to radiate through the pores and beyond, farther and farther. Touch other vibrations, give them identification, penetrate them, and go on. Finally, contact an immense vibrating thought. Contemplate its nature, its size, its ramifications; then, absorb it through your vibrating feelers, drawing it in to your original body circumscription — slowly, slowly — then, digest it.

Could you write this experience and describe the thought encountered? Could you adapt the thought to some useful purpose?

Using sight.

Sight is the most mental and the most versatile of the senses; yet, it calls generously on the other senses to make its imagery fulfilling.

Imagine a landscape: trees, grass, patches of flowers, a stream, and sunshine streaking through the foliage. Lie down in the middle of the grassy field; then with your own inventiveness, create the smells, the tastes, the feel, the sight of all around you. Slowly, let each of these sense responses enter into your entire awareness, each a separate awareness, yet a coordinate whole. Become conscious that the scene is changing. Create your own changes — a different planet, the center of the earth, the bottom of the ocean — but let the acute-sense syndrome change with you.

Go gently and slowly. Hold and experience these changes. Relax and sink back into your ordinary state. What did you bring with you? Could you paint it, write it, or put it to some extraordinary purpose?

The whole man.

THE FOREGOING — body image and body awareness — contains a few suggestions for developing and integrating potentials of children that they may more fully serve their own purpose and the purposes of humanity. Wise teachers know that suggestions are merely prods to start the concept rolling. From there, ideas more pertinent to the individual child and the individual circumstance are adapted, innovated, expanded, or diminished as progress indicates. Also, because wise teachers "read" children more creatively, they no longer consider the inconsistently functioning children in their classrooms as inexplicable problems; they recognize them as youngsters in need of further help in development.

In education, the whole-child concept of the past revolved around portions of the body image — physical structure, rational mental growth. Today, the concept of the whole man is emerging: body image and body awareness; physical, emotional, mental, spiritual.[19] Wherever this concept is practiced, over the entire earth, problem children disappear and functioning, developing youngsters emerge.

REFERENCES

Brown, Norman O. "The Place of Mystery in the Life of the Mind," *Harper's Magazine* (May 1961).

Combs, Arthur W. "What Can Man Become?" *California Journal for Instructional Improvement* (December 1961).

---

[19] Kuniyoshi Obara, *op. cit.*

SENSORY-MOTOR

Ellington, Careth. *The Shadow Children.* Chicago, Ill.: Topaz Books, 1968.

Haeusserman, Else. *Developmental Potential of Preschool Children.* New York, N.Y.: Grune and Stratton, 1958.

Gesell, A. *Infancy and Human Growth.* New York, N.Y.: MacMillan, 1940.

Korzybski, Alfred. *Science and Sanity.* New York, N.Y.: The International Non-Aristotelian Library Publishing Company, 1958.

Krech, David. "The Chemistry of Learning," *Saturday Review* (January 20, 1968).

Miles, Helen Cabot. "Design for Tomorrow," *Art Education* (December 1964).

Nielsen, Johannes M. *Agnosia, Apraxia, Aphasia.* New York, N.Y.: Harper Brothers, 1959.

——————.*Mind Blindness.* New York, N.Y.: Harper Brothers, 1960.

Piaget, Jean. *The Origin of Intelligence in Children.* New York, N.Y.: W. W. Norton, 1963.

——————.*The Child's Concept of the World.* New York, N.Y.: Harcourt Bruce, 1929.

Sorokin, Pitirim A. "Three Basic Trends of Our Times: The Factors Which Are Creating a New World Culture," *Main Currents in Modern Thought* (January, March 1960).

Thomas, Hobart F. *Education for Self Awareness.* New York, N.Y.: Psychosynthesis Research Foundation, 1966.

White, Burton L. *Experience in Early Human Development.* New York, N.Y.: Oxford University Press, 1965.

The creativity of a teacher is apparent when she begins to build a program using what is nearest in meaning to the child. By organizing a sequence of activities, by reviewing and reinforcing the material to be learned in interesting ways, and by making it concrete and real she will know that the children are truly ready for each new step.

— **Eunice Sharp**
"Creativity in Arithmetic for E.H. Children,"
Teaching Educationally Handicapped Children
(San Rafael, Calif.: Academic Therapy Publications, 1967.)

Tactile-Kinesthetic Approaches to Learning

Lena L. Gitter

———•———

THE MONTESSORI method, primarily educative, is designed to teach children who fall within the wide range of normal ability and behavior. It is also therapeutic, however, and serves admirably to reach those children who need special attention because of mental or emotional difficulties which cannot be dealt with in the course of a non-Montessori educational program. Children with reading difficulties certainly qualify as needing a therapeutic program which can get at the roots of their failure. In what way can the Montessori method do this?

To answer the question, it is necessary to consider some of the reasons for reading failure. There are the physiological reasons: minimal brain dysfunction, dyslexia, slow physical development, or eye problems, such as amblyopia or myopia, which may go undetected. Even when these conditions are corrected, however, psychological problems associated with repeated failure remain to be handled. Thus, we can consider that these children require therapeutic assistance similar to that needed by children who are reading failures for psychological reasons. These reasons might include the desire to punish their parents, to retreat from competitive situations, or to resist attempts to measure themselves against real challenges.

Such children may or may not be receiving psychological help. The Montessori method, however, can offer, in an educational setting, therapeutic assistance quite apart from additional psychological treatment, because certain aspects built into the method are designed to neutralize those pressures which prevent a child from achieving success in reading after an experience of prior failure.

In the context of reading failure, the most important aspect of the Montessori method is its "programing for success." Each exercise, each piece of equipment is so designed that the child can correct his own mistakes and experience success. One example, shown in detail later in this paper, involves exercises with various types of cylinders. Working with the cylinders prepares the child's muscles for writing; at the same time, he is experiencing success in placing each cylinder in its proper place. If he errs, he is left with a space and a cylinder which do not fit together and he can remove the cylinders and rearrange them by himself without pressure, public exposure, or a teacher urging him on. No matter how long it takes, he will eventually succeed in matching cylinders and spaces correctly.

SENSORY-MOTOR

The nature of the Montessori materials and exercises also makes the method noncompetitive; each child works alone at his own pace and there is no opportunity for invidious comparisons. There is no need for grouping or for class awareness that one child cannot keep up with the rest. There is no reading aloud to the assembled group, a practice which is daily torture for the poor reader. While the other children are busily engaged with individual tasks, there is time for the teacher to listen to each child read only to her. Montessori did not prescribe any basal readers or texts; the variety of books available for the child to look at, to discuss with the teacher, and to read makes allowance for the differing tastes of children.

The following exercises may seem remote from the teaching of reading. In the Montessori method, however, reading is not taught "out of the blue" but as part of an integrated, graduated program of education designed to prepare the whole child. The indirect preparation is of great importance, since its aim is to create in the child a good feeling about himself and his abilities. Without this good feeling he lacks confidence, he may not try to read, he may avoid challenges, and he will probably be prepared for the failure which will inevitably come to confirm his prophecies. Continual achievement, in a graded series of tasks performed at the child's own speed and without the pressure of competition, is the best guarantee of a healthy self-concept which will enable the child to attack the task of reading with confidence, enthusiasm, and the expectation of further success.

Even before the didactic materials are introduced, however, certain other lessons are absorbed by the children in a Montessori classroom. The children first learn to control their bodily movements. They must learn to move among the tables and chairs without breaking them or making noise, for if they cannot handle these relatively large and sturdy objects with care and assurance, how can they profit from the more complex and fragile materials to which they will be introduced? At the very start, then, the teacher makes certain that the children have sufficient control to be able to use them satisfactorily.

Grace and courtesy.

THE LESSONS classified as Grace and Courtesy Experiences may be considered the ground rules of classroom behavior. The children are taught respect for other people and regard for the dignity of others — behavior based on an understanding of one's own dignity and value. Manners are our way of demonstrating this regard. For example, there are lessons in which the children learn to greet one another politely. Carrying a water glass (first an empty one and then a filled one) on a tray, the child walks a short distance and presents the glass to another child. This child receives it graciously and carries it to a third child. The children are taught to sit in their chairs properly and quietly for a few minutes and then to rise and seat themselves again. They learn to move about the room with security and ease.

Some schools serve milk or juice and cookies. Setting the tables, serving the food, washing the dishes, and other duties are all performed with great delight by the children. Each morning or each week, the waitresses, table setters, and dishwashers are chosen or assigned. As soon as the youngest children have learned to safely carry a glass on a tray, they are eligible for the waiter's job. The same command of the muscles which makes the little waitresses skillful at their work also enables the children at the table to hold their knives, forks, or spoons properly. This success, in turn, develops poise and confidence.

Silence exercises.

Montessori developed techniques for encouraging concentration and self-discipline. She emphasized silence as a profound experience which can be taught through the Silence Exercises. In learning control and mastery of themselves through these exercises, children become calmer and better able to assimilate learning. The exercises that call for self-control, attention, and coordination of muscles teach the children the complete meaning of silence. The exercises give the teacher an opportunity to check the child's hearing and to help him formulate good listening habits.

Education of the senses.

LEARNING requires concentration. The only way the child can concentrate is to fix his attention on a task he is performing with his hands. Conscious knowledge is obtained by comparing and discriminating between the impressions received by the senses. Acquisition of the various sense perceptions is usually done casually and in a haphazard manner, but the Montessori apparatus are designed to enable the child to acquire the knowledge systematically so that the order is apparent.

From the time of ancient Greece, the world's greatest educators, including Plato and Aristotle, have recognized the value of coordinating sensory and mental training. Montessori placed great emphasis upon the education of the senses. This is accomplished through the use of sensorial materials.

Manipulation of simple forms.

The knobbed cylinders are among the first objects to be presented to the children. (See Figure 1.) Each set contains ten cylinders which are fitted into a wooden box. All of the cylinders are of solid wood, each with a little button at the top for taking them out and putting them back into the holes in the box. There are four sets of cylinders. In the first set, the pieces are all of equal length, but they are graduated in diameter. In the second set, they are all of the same diameter and are graduated in height. The pieces in the third set vary in both height and diameter, the cylindrical form alone remaining constant. In the fourth set, height and diameter vary in reverse order to that of the third set.

Montessori adapted these cylinders in order to utilize the instinct children seem to have for arranging small objects in rows. In playing with the cylinders, the child takes them all out, mixes them up on the table, and then puts them back, each cylinder going back into the hole into which it fits. Since the big cylinders will not go into the little hole and the tall cylinders will not go into the shallow holes, the child soon calculates the proper place for each cylinder. After the child can do this easily and perfectly, he will still continue, many times, to empty out his cylinders and put them back. The finger muscles grow secure through handling the cylinders, and the child exercises his sense of touch

SENSORY-MOTOR

Figure 1.

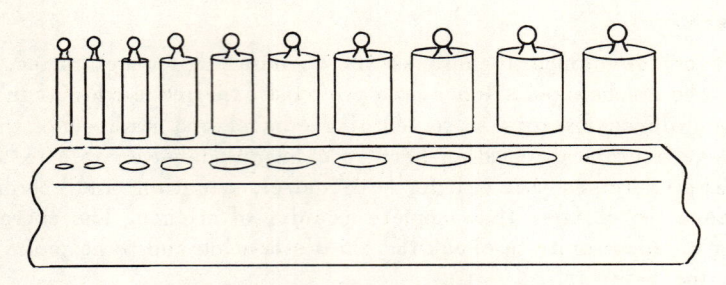

Set No. 1: Cylinders vary in diameter.

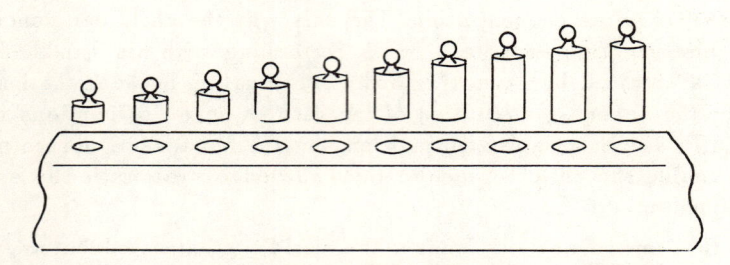

Set No. 2: Cylinders vary in height.

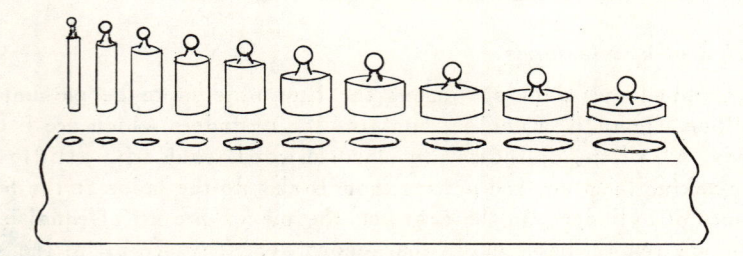

Set No. 3: Cylinders vary in height and diameter.

Set No. 4: Cylinders vary in height and diameter.

Figure 2.

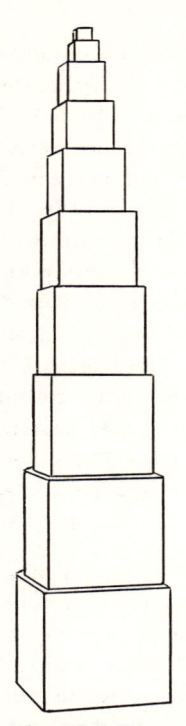

The Pink Tower

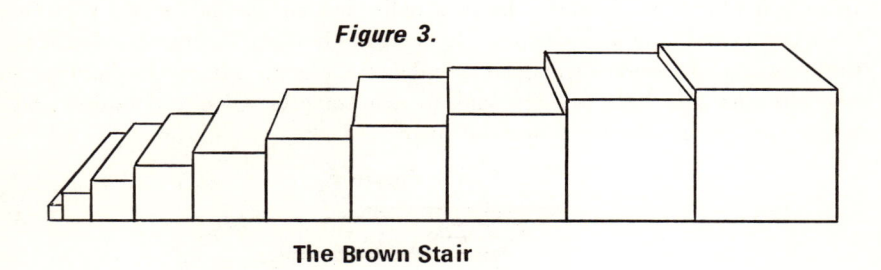

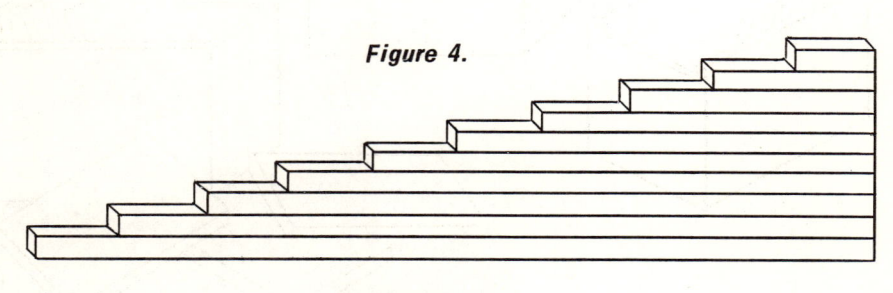

Figure 3.

The Brown Stair

Figure 4.

The Red Rods

67

SENSORY-MOTOR

by first running his finger around each cylinder and then around its hole before slipping it into its place.

Other simple devices which are presented to the very young children are the graduated cubes (the Pink Tower), the graduated rectangular blocks (the Brown Stair), and the series of rods (the Red Rods). The Pink Tower is made from ten blocks which are graded from one centimeter to ten centimeters. (See Figure 2.) The child builds both vertically and horizontally with the blocks. The Brown Stair is also constituted of ten blocks. (See Figure 3.) It has the same cross section as the Pink Tower. Together, these two exercises allow for over seventy patterned combinations. The Brown Stair can also be constructed vertically, and the blocks can be interspersed with Pink Tower blocks to make a tower over six feet tall. The Red Rods graduate equally in length from ten centimeters to one hundred centimeters (one meter). (See Figure 4.) The child mixes the ten rods up on the rug and reassembles them in a "long stair" pattern. He learns sensorially the idea of short, long, shorter, longer, and he experiences equal gradation, a fundamental mathematical concept.

The baric sense.

The Baric Tablets consist of a series of wooden tablets by which the children learn to discriminate between the weights of two different objects. (See Figure 5.) The tablets are made of wood of four different qualities, and they differ in weight by about one-fifth of an ounce. First, the child takes a tablet in each hand. The two tablets differ noticeably in weight, and the child balances them on his palms until he becomes fully conscious of the difference between the heavier and the lighter. After he has learned to discriminate the difference in weight of the two tablets, he is blindfolded and he takes two tablets at a time from the mixed pile before him. He weighs them in his hands, deciding whether there is any difference in their weight. He places all of the heavier tablets in one pile and all of the lighter ones in another pile. Often, of course, he gets two heavy tablets or two light ones at once.

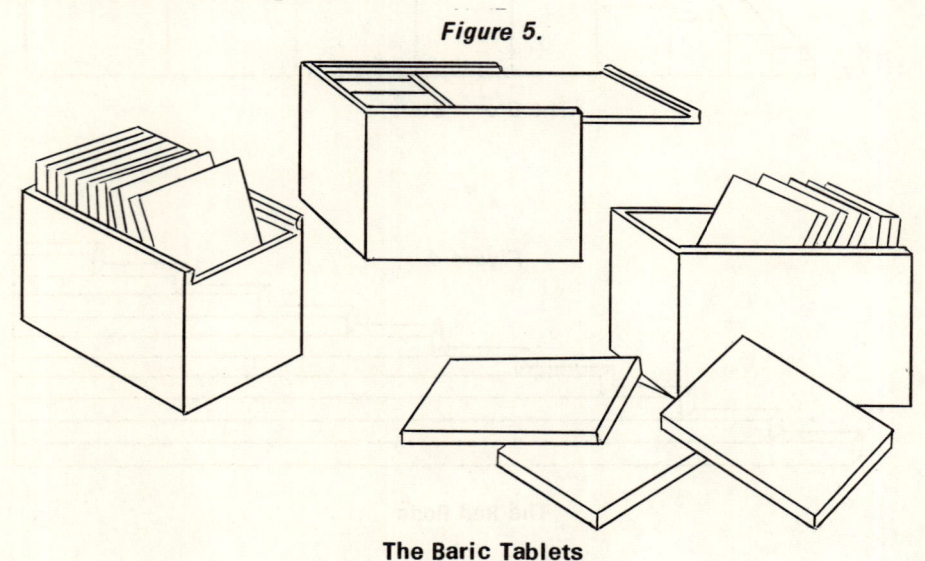

Figure 5.

The Baric Tablets

68

The sense of touch.

WHILE WORKING among her deficient children, Montessori became impressed by the keenness of the sense of touch of children under five. After that time in a child's life this particular sense seems to become slightly dulled and less amenable to education. Montessori begins her discussion on the education of the senses with the suggestion that the first exercise should be that of washing the hands. Since the only method of training the sense of touch is by passing the fingertips over the surfaces of objects, the hands should be scrupulously clean. Washing thoroughly with warm water and soap, the children then rinse their hands in cold water and dry them.

The first of the tactile exercises, and one which eventually leads to writing, employs two small boards, twelve by six and one-half inches in size, called Touch Boards. (See Figure 6.) The boards are finished with alternating sandpaper and polished surfaces, and the child learns to identify, with a light touch, the qualities of *rough* and *smooth*. The practice of isolating the sense of touch by blindfolding the child or having him shut his eyes makes the sense of touch much more acute.

Figure 6.

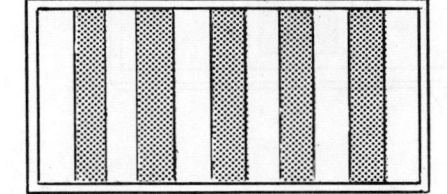

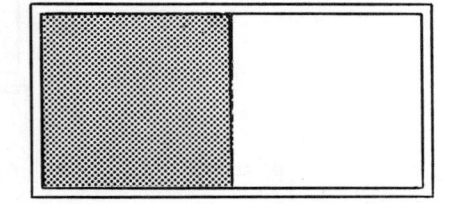

Touch Boards

Another method for training the sense of touch is to use a large variety of squares of cloth. We use two squares of each material: two of the various kinds and qualities of silk; two of every sort of woolen goods, from the coarsest tweed to the finest flannel; various grades of cotton; linen; and so on, until nearly every sort of clothing material in common use is represented. The exercise in teaching these materials begins with two strongly contrasting textures. A child is given, for instance, a square of velvet and a square of silk. He is taught to feel the difference between the two fabrics and is then asked to pick out from a mixed pile of the squares on the table in front of him the duplicate of each of the two. At first he is not required to learn the name of the material but only to recognize its quality by feeling it with his fingers. However, he rapidly acquires a knowledge of all of the different kinds of material in the boxes.

Indirect preparation for writing.

Following the exercises in the sense of touch, activities with geometrical insets are introduced. The blue wooden geometrical plane forms, of different sizes, are made to fit into square blue wooden frames. (See Figure 7.) Each inset is easily removed from the frame by a button fixed in the center. The child puts the inset into the frame; later he matches it with three outlines on white cardboard. This is an exercise in discrimination of size and one-to-one correspon-

SENSORY-MOTOR

dence. Through this activity, the child's already trained sense of touch learns to follow a great variety of contours — a decided step toward the art of writing.

Figure 7.

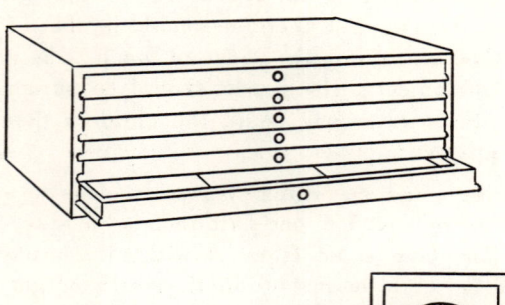

Geometric Cabinet and Insets

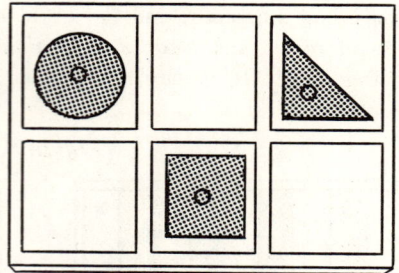

The mechanics of writing.

WHEN MONTESSORI was working with exceptional children, she observed that manipulation of the pen was one of the most difficult skills for these children to learn. After the children had learned to trace the letters with their fingers and to know them by sight, they still did not have the ability to copy them correctly because their muscles were not sufficiently well trained to hold and direct a pen or pencil. The deficient children overcame the difficulty of handling a pencil by first tracing, with little sticks, letters that were cut out of wood.

For normal children, however, Montessori devised a series of geometrical forms made with metal insets. (See Figure 8.) The shapes, which fit into stands, are placed on the paper, and the child, using pencils in two colors, traces inside the frame and then around the inset. He then fills in the space inside the controlled lines. Patterns with varied designs and colors can be made with these insets, and the activity also leads to the discovery of the similarity of block letters to geometric forms. (See Figure 9.)

Through these exercises, the child acquires the muscular coordination necessary to follow contours with precision and firmness. He is master of his pencil and can control the direction and weight of the lines.

Sandpaper letters.

The purpose of using sandpaper letters is to help the child to learn to recognize the forms of letters by touch and sight as well as by their sounds. Gaining

TACTILE-KINESTHETIC APPROACHES

Figure 8.

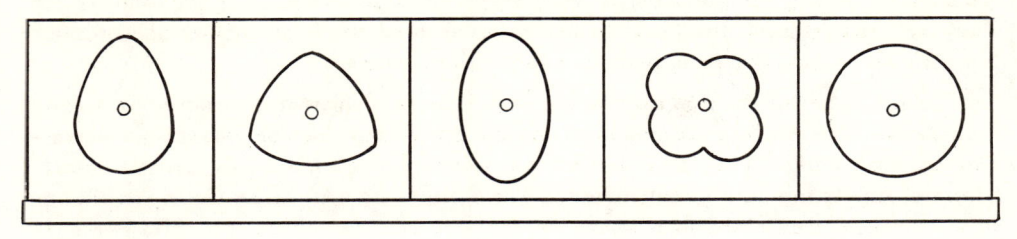

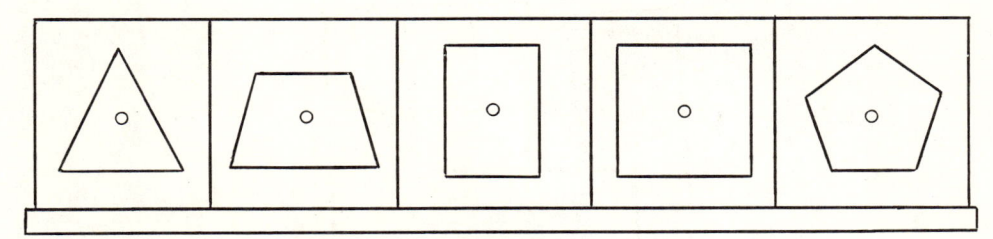

Metal Insets

Figure 9.

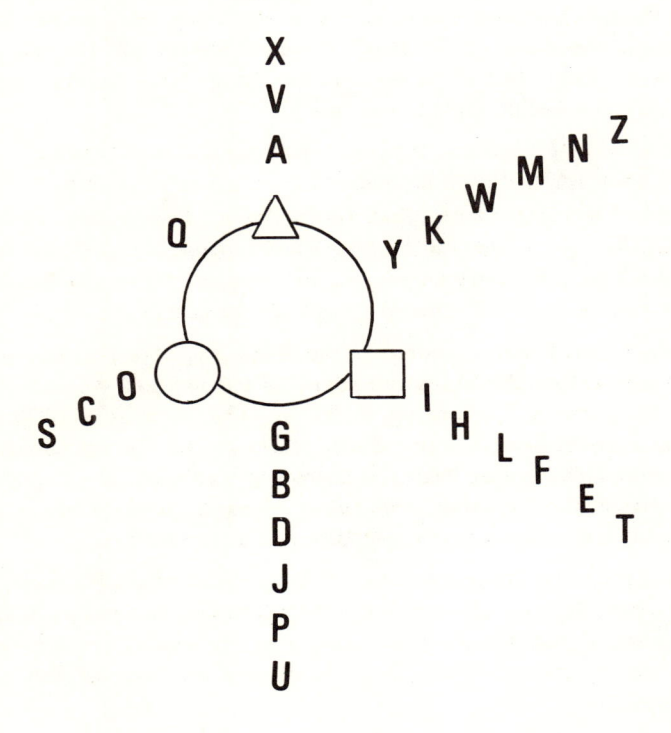

Relation of Block Letters to Geometric Forms

71

muscular memory of the form of the letters through touch is a preparation for writing, and it helps the child to better understand the composition of words as he begins to analyze them and their component sounds.

Each letter of the alphabet is cut from fine sandpaper and mounted on strong cardboard. The vowels are mounted on blue cards and the consonants are mounted on pink cards. The large letters are mounted on large cards and the small letters are mounted on smaller cards. The letters are placed on the right side of the cards so that there is a space on the left side by which the child can hold the card.

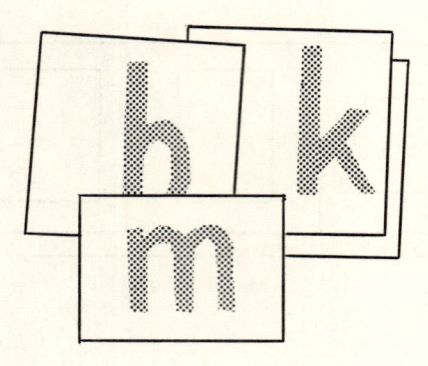

When teaching the child to feel the letter, great care must be taken to see that he starts where one would normally start in writing and to see that he traces the letter in the direction in which it would be written. He must keep his fingers on the letter from start to finish, except for the dots on the *i* and *j*, the cross on the *f* where the script alphabet is used.

In teaching the letters, the teacher may select, for example, *A* and *C*. Taking the card upon which the *A* is mounted, she gives it to the child, and pronounces the sound of the letter with great distinctness. Taking the child's hand, she then shows him how to follow the contour of the letter with his two forefingers — just as he would do if he were writing it. At the same time, she has him pronounce it. In these first lessons, the child learns the phonetic sound of the letter.

When *C* has been presented in the same way, the teacher puts the two cards on the table before the child and says, "Give me *C*." When he has done so, she says, "Give me *A*." Pointing to the *C*, she then asks, "What is this?" She shows him again how to trace each letter, giving its sound as he does so, and then leaves him to play with the letters by himself. By the time the child has learned the entire alphabet, the sound of each letter is associated in his mind with the muscular movements necessary to reproduce it.

Variations may be introduced as the child is ready for them. For example, he can be blindfolded so that he learns to recognize the shape of the letters solely by touch. Such modifications and additions, however, should come only after he has thoroughly mastered the basic exercises and has gained the confidence of achievement.

In working with the sandpaper letters, the child is learning to reproduce letter forms through sensory imagery — visual, auditory, tactile, and kinesthetic.

- The child sees the letter.
- The child hears the letter's name as the teacher pronounces it.
- The child repeats the letter. (This auditory feedback is important.)
- Tracing the letter with two fingers, the child gets a tactile image.
- Tracing the letter while blindfolded adds a kinesthetic image.

The movable alphabet.

ONCE THE CHILD has mastered the sounds and shapes of the letters of the alphabet, he is ready for the next step in his direct preparation for reading and writing. All too often, actual writing must wait until the child has gained sufficient muscular control to handle a pencil, and with the special child — as with some normal children — small-muscle control is delayed until beyond the age when the child is actually emotionally and mentally ready for working with words. The movable alphabet thus becomes the appropriate tool for bridging the gap between readiness for writing and the ability to use the pencil.

The letters of the movable alphabet are cut out of cardboard in two colors, using the same colors as were used for the sandpaper letters — blue for the vowels and pink for the consonants. Thus, the child learns that the letters are divided into two groups. There are several duplicates of each letter. The letters are kept in a box with each letter placed in its own compartment. At the bottom of each compartment is pasted a copy of the letter that belongs there. This enables the child to place his letters in the correct compartment when he is finished with them.

In working with the movable alphabet, use pictures or models of objects that have phonetic names. Suggest a three-letter word that is related to the picture or object to the child and, by sound analysis, break it into its component parts. Say to the child, "Now let's pick out the letters." Take the letters out of the compartments one at a time, pronouncing the sound as you do so. Place the letters before the child in sequential order. Continue building more monosyllabic words until ten or more examples of each vowel sound have been built or until the child tires. Polysyllabic words will follow at a later time. Make sure that the child realizes that the word symbolizes, explains, or is a nominal definition of the picture or object.

With the movable alphabet, the child can reproduce words he has read, he can form the words he speaks, he can compose his own stories, and he can read these stories aloud as part of his work in reading. He experiences a sense of achievement as he understands that he can compose words and sentences that other people — his teacher, his parents, his friends — can read. He can communicate with others via the printed word.

Once again we are able to cultivate both the immediate goal — formation of words and sentences — and the long-range goal of developing the child's self-image in a positive and favorable way.

The explosion into writing.

The sandpaper letters and the movable alphabet help the child develop the

SENSORY-MOTOR

following skills necessary for handwriting: eye-hand coordination; associating letter names with their form; associating capital and small letter forms; associating type and manuscript forms; learning similarities and differences in letter forms; and developing memory of letter forms through the sensory imagery discussed above.

The sequence of activities which leads to writing is as follows:

• The child's fingertips have been taught to touch objects understandingly through the various tactile materials.

• Sensitivity and comprehension in the palms of the child's hands have been awakened by lifting the tablets of different weights.

• The geometric insets have helped the child understand form. When he puts his fingers around the edge of a square or a triangle, a forward step is made toward the real sensation of form.

• Montessori says that coloring in the geometrical forms is more preparation for writing than is filling in dozens of pages of the old-time copy books.

• With the sandpaper alphabet the child learns to associate the sound of the letter with its form.

• The movable alphabet allows the child to begin forming words, phrases, and sentences from the letters of the alphabet.

The explosion into reading.

BEFORE the child reads, he must speak — just as before he spoke, he had to hear. Now the process goes on and the teacher must spend much time speaking with the child (especially if the child is in any way maternally deprived). She must ask him *when, who, what, where, why,* and *how* in conversation lessons. By trying to answer the questions, the child builds concepts into his vocabulary. A story may be built in this manner, too.

The teacher also reads and tells stories and poems to the children. At this time, the child can build an attitude of respect for books, especially if there is a book corner in the classroom and a practical life exercise is given in how to turn a page, etc. In all these lessons, the child should be encouraged to speak before the group. This can be done by having him relate experiences or explain a drawing.

The sequence which leads to reading is as follows:

• The child hears the word that he has just built from the movable alphabet being phonetically sounded out.

• He matches the word built from the movable alphabet to the corresponding picture or model.

• He sees the teacher write on paper the sounds that match the word previously built.

• He realizes that the built word and the written word have the same meaning because they match the same picture or object.

• He matches a new label to a picture without the use of the movable alphabet.

TACTILE-KINESTHETIC APPROACHES

A MONTESSORI LABELING EXERCISE

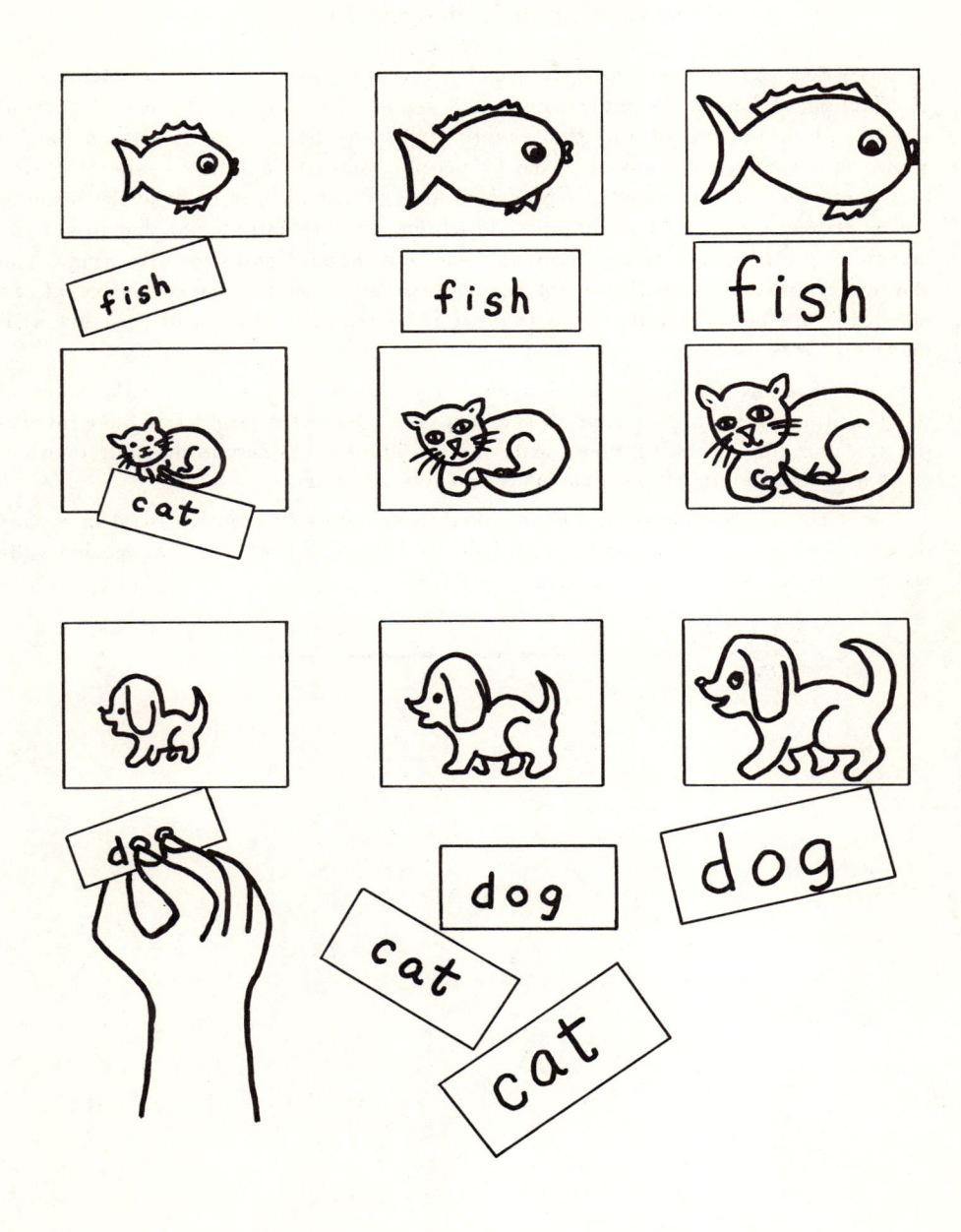

SENSORY-MOTOR

- The exercise is repeated as often as the child wishes.
- The shelves are labeled for each piece of apparatus.
- Each child's chair is labeled with his name.
- Every object in the room is labeled with its name.
- Objects are labeled with their corresponding color.

IN PRESENTING these materials and activities which are used in Montessori teaching, I hasten to explain that this is by no means an attempt to present the complete picture of the Montessori approach. Rather, it is only a partial answer to the question asked of me by people who are looking for specific aids that can be put to immediate practical use. I have chosen to describe some of the most basic materials in the order in which they are introduced, but to get the complete picture, one would have to take advanced Montessori training. The Montessori materials still are not readily available on the market; some of the apparatus are being manufactured in the United States, but most of them are still imported from Europe.

An imaginative teacher who is capable with her hands could make some of the teaching aids which I have described. Other teachers might find that involving the parents in making these materials is helpful in increasing their involvement and interest in all aspects of the school program.

It's not necessary to be a championship swimmer to enjoy a swim in a pond on a summer's day, so I want to conclude by inviting all of you: "Come in — the water's fine."

Relating Body Awareness
and Effortless Motion
to Visual Training

C. V. Lyons
Emily Bradley Lyons

AS THE PACE and rhythms accelerate in this runaway world, can we learn to interpret, to live with the rushing blur of movement and tempo? Can we learn to match our self-motion with our environmental motion, our interior heartbeat with the external pulse pounding around us? Can we learn to create our own island of peace in the midst of turmoil? How can we learn to use motion to serve us — to increase our awareness, our imagination, our understanding, our fine thinking? How can we use it to free us rather than allowing it to destroy us?

These are questions that must be asked in the heart and mind of every thoughtful person. These are questions that remain in our minds during an optometric evaluation, guiding our search for answers to human problems, as we measure and study movement patterns through our probes of visual analyses and visual abilities.

When these visual movements — the refinements of movement learned throughout the body — show us imbalances, restrictions, and tensions, we can be certain of finding them if the person brings a history of limitations and problems in reading, writing, spelling, mathematics, or other areas of symbolic thinking.

When we optometrically evaluate children with neurological handicaps or children who show educational handicaps with no measurable neurological involvement, we build "feelers" of sensitivity to problems shared with all human beings. Because these youngsters' difficulties represent exaggerated adjustments to living, revealed in an obvious and dramatic way, they spotlight the puzzling, sublimated problems of the average, or normal, child. Barriers are removed that prevent the potentially superior child from achieving the promise within him. In adults, problems are exposed that have been long and carefully repressed and blindly accepted as inevitable realities of living to which one must adjust.

Whether these problems exist in child or adult, in exaggerated or sublimated form, we know that difficulty in symbolic thinking is rooted in failure to build firm and deep anchors in individual sensory-motor skills, in failure to match and correlate these movements between systems, and in failure to refine these matching patterns so that vision, through its own fine matching movements, emerges as a gethering center for all movement systems. Actions, feelings, or events in time or space from all other systems are translated into visual symbols in this center. This process requires minimum energy to release maximum information. If this fine matching between systems fails, fine thinking for symbols will fail also.

As we study an individual's case history, his analysis, and his abilities and performance tests, our thinking is guided by the concept of vision as a dynamic, functioning part of a whole person. We are not studying an isolated set of camera lenses located in the head. Our understanding is influenced by functional concepts, developed long ago through the Optometric Extension Program Foundation, Duncan, Oklahoma, with emphasis on the inseparable relationship between visual and bodily movement patterns. The role of vision as a generator of creative, innovative, productive thinking (thinking through visualization) is our guiding "search model" for locating the sensory-motor delays, the "hollows," or the mismatches that have pervasively restricted or blocked the individual's visual shifting.[1] We know that wherever we find these adverse patterns, the person must remodel his visual and motor worlds, building new patterns of movement. We know that this remodeling must be a guided, directed program.[2] It must be a program that is not satisfied merely by building large or gross movement awareness, performed at high-effort level. It must be directed toward building increasing awareness of fine changes. Fine kinesthetic awareness is not possible at high-effort level.

TODAY, more than ever before, movement studies and movement programs play a leading role in many fields devoted to child education or guidance. The current preoccupation with physical fitness, exercise, and developmental programs — a violent oscillation away from the former universal avoidance of any self-motion — creates a paradox in the thinking about the role of exercise. If the concept of a motor program is that success is directly related to the amount of energy expended (the more vigorous the action, the more panting and perspiring that is demonstrated, the better the exercise), the program may appear to be somewhat successful. It may appear most successful when used with children who show developmental delays or environmental deprivations that have limited their early motor development; any method containing movement would be expected to bring some improvement. If, however, learning is to match and relate to higher forms of abstract learning, so that learning plateaus are not reached, from the beginning of the training program our attention must be directed more toward how the exercise is done and how much effort is used to do it than to the result of the exercise.

---

[1] C. V. Lyons and Emily B. Lyons, "A Search Model for Optometry." Paper delivered at the West Coast Visual Training Conference, Seaside Oregon, 1957. Transcripts of this paper and others from the visual-training conferences mentioned in this article are available from Dr. Caryl Croisant, 465 Kern Street, Morro Bay, California 93422.

[2] A. M. Skeffington, "Optometric Training: Rationale and Goals." Paper delivered at the St. Louis Conference on Theoretical Optometry and Visual Training, St. Louis, Missouri, January 1967.

In essence, any exercise should be a demonstration of the effortlessness that is learned in the substructures and that allow that particular movement to happen. In developing a program for an individual, if we are directed by this thought, we will not rush into activities that demand movement concepts which the person has never learned as balanced, effortless processing. If we present him with an activity that is too difficult to perform with ease and balance, we allow him no alternatives except to refuse to comply or to perform under increased tension. Rather, we should choose sequential activities that bring increased awareness of balanced, supported movement, release from tension, and economy of energy. As the person's movements grow in freedom, his understanding grows so that even vigorous movement can still be calm and he can think and create wherever he is or whatever he is doing. He can find his own island of peace.

In an optometric training program designed to build flexibility and freedom in visual-motor movement patterns through detection of fine differences between patterns, one of the basic steps in gaining those freedoms is learning repose while moving. For anyone — child or adult — living in our accelerated society, this is a difficult concept to learn. It is especially difficult for a learning-disabled child whose exteriorizations of tensions range from a state of compulsive perpetual motion to the opposite extreme — rigid resistance to moving himself.

Regardless of how they exteriorize, these children are expressing themselves as human beings who are out of balance with themselves and their environment. They have not matched their interior movement, pulse, or rhythm with the exterior surge, beat, and tempo in the world around them. They have never listened to their own muscles, felt their own rhythms, looked at their own mind's pictures. They must be guided in learning from the wisest tutor anyone can have — their own bodies.

The most effective way of starting this "tutoring" from awareness of one's body is to lie on the back on a firm, flat surface. The floor is preferable because it provides the largest area of support beneath the body. On the floor, the tensions existing in the upright position, because of body imbalances and resistance to falling, are reduced to a minimum. Here, directed awareness can be given to each segment of the body, allowing it to find supported rest beneath. Accomplishing this is difficult for many people who have difficulty differentiating between balanced and imbalanced movements, who have unknowingly "muscled" in the upright position for so long that they continue these same tensions when they are lying down. This is especially difficult for many learning-disabled children with movement tensions. Because, in the human body, immobility is more difficult to learn than is mobility, these children tenaciously resist lying down during daylight hours, continuing their incessant activity into nightfall. When exhausted parents are ready to collapse into bed, the child's compulsive energy seems inexhaustible. If we hope to lead him into the refinements of mobile movement, to help him to find balance between the extremes of propulsive, frenzied activity and flabby lethargy, he must learn the opposite of mobility — rest through immobile, supported balance.

A record produced by Jane Brown, "The Art of Dance and Relaxation," offers an effective technique for learning to relax through supported balance.[3] Specific instructions are provided for developing body awareness — learning to release from tension by finding the support beneath and throughout the body. Since parents need repose as much as do the youngsters, they should be encouraged to work along with their children. If they, too, absorb the ideas into their minds through their bodies, they can more readily translate these thoughts to their children, and thus more wisely guide them. They will understand the importance of learning effortless balance within themselves, and they will learn the value of spending some time each day becoming better acquainted with themselves.

The nonstop jet-propelled child, who actively resists pausing "on the floor," must be calmly, quietly, and firmly encouraged to make dynamic rest a part of his daily program. He should be started slowly and consistently, with one minute of directed awareness the first day, increasing the time by one minute the following day, and so on, until he finds it a comforting and stabilizing time and is gradually able to hear what his muscles are telling him.

As the ideas from the record become part of his and his parents' thinking, on some days he should be encouraged to work without the record. He may give verbal instructions himself, or he might talk to his mother (or any person sharing his quiet time), guiding her in how to rest. While he is lying on the floor, we can also help him to understand the support received from the floor and how this support, if he will use it, helps him to move his arms and legs with a minimum of energy. If he does not learn to move his extensors effortlessly, he will continue muscling and hoisting with arms and legs in bursts of speed that require maximum energy.

FLUID, sustained action is accomplished when the natural supports of the body are used in balanced relationship to gravity. Dance therapists Milton Fehr and Jane Brown have created a system of relaxed movement based on this philosophy. From them we adapt the idea of "float," when working with arms, to "suggest the absence of effort and enable one to experience the fact that at every point in the movement the arm is supported by the shoulder socket."[4] We use this same idea of supported resting for moving the legs; the children find their support at the hip joint, which in turn extends the support of the floor.

These movements, using arms and legs, and which are learned on the floor, can be carried into "on-all-fours" activities through rocking on hands and knees, crawling, creeping, then rolling, where the continuing feeling of support of hands and toes beneath the body allows the movement to gain in the graceful, sinuous feline quality of balanced movement.[5] No exercise should be given that is not directing attention to the "four squareness" and balanced unity of the body.

---

[3] This LP record is available from Miss Brown, 3301 North Main Street, Pleasant Hill, California.

[4] Milton Fehr, "Dance Therapy for Polio Patients," *Dance Magazine*, n.d.

[5] Jane Brown, *Manual for Effortless Motion* (In press).

These same principles can be related sequentially into sitting effortlessly, as a child must do for long periods at school and as an adult must do at an office desk — the places where body and visual warps are built. The person must practice finding the support of the chair beneath by resting the body into it evenly — rotating the pelvic area down into the seat and back toward the spine. When this resting position is found, the trunk will feel securely supported and the arms will feel light and released, gaining the ease to relate to fingers for the fine movements necessary for writing. The head and neck will release, and the eyes will find their own "eye level," all with greater freedom of movement. Unless a person has found this rested, supported, well-seated position, it is useless to demand that he "sit up straight." If he is requested to do so, he will comply simply by increasing his tensions through muscling and holding himself rigidly erect.

As movements learned on the floor are carried into sitting, we are refining the movements for achieving that unique posture and locomotion of the human body — the erect carriage — a position of joy when moving freely or of despair when restricted. The ability to stand, walk, run, jump — to achieve all the flexible movements of the upright carriage — depends on finding and using the solid support of the earth beneath the body from the equal balance and full use of the two feet. As the feet, legs, and pelvic area match their movements and relate, they rotate evenly outward, forming a solid pillar of support for finding our midline — our personal zero starting point for making all spatial estimations. When standing freely, the trunk rests on the legs just as easily as it rests when seated on a chair. All activities and exercises in the upright position are demonstrations of learning this principle of balance.

We use the effortlessness of arm and leg movements accomplished on the floor to match movements in the upright position. Whirling windmill movements with arms can demonstrate the ease of arm movement. Reciprocity of arms becomes possible for youngsters previously unable to straighten or cross arms overhead without hoisting and straining shoulders, back, and neck. Moving arms easily in the upright position results from rested shoulder support as well as from continued awareness of the downward rotation of the pelvic area related to the feet.

Any work at the chalkboard is a demonstration of this learned ability. That arms make circles, lines, or letters in the process of moving is simply a pictorial trail of how well or poorly the arms have moved. When a person gains understanding of this, he can observe and analyze his own chalk outlines to find out if he has moved under error and tension. In this way, he can determine the imbalances that need to be corrected.

WALKING must be learned through the thought of placing one foot in front of the other. There should be a continuing awareness of the equal and supported balance of the body so that during forward motion (as the moving foot passes from back to front in a direct forward alignment with the other foot) the body rests continuously as if on two feet. Milton Fehr describes it well: "In a perfect gait, the trunk, or upper part of your body, does not work at all. It rides the moving the moving legs as a fine horseman rides his steed — sitting with graceful ease, letting the animal do the work."[6]

As the working foot moves down — contacting the floor sequentially from heel through all the toes, placing the body securely on the supporting leg and foot — the body continues the downward movement. In this way, movement is continuously, directly forward, uncomplicated by falling from side to side or jogging up and down, which would require twice as much energy to move the same distance. M. Feldenkrais tells us:

> Perfect maturity of the antigravity function is recognizable by the narrowness of gait. The traces left by the feet when advancing fit between two parallel lines, about two-thirds of the width of both feet, apart. . . . The legs move simply, *i.e.*, they do not do anything else but the movement strictly necessary for the purpose. So does the whole body.[7]

When *how* to walk is understood, the flexibility and effortlessness of it can be demonstrated by activities on the walking beam. With increased refinements in matching patterns, the individual is freed to understand and use programing, sequencing, and all the other refinements for efficient walking and running.

Effortless jumping skill cannot be accomplished until the refined series of movement patterns necessary for this skill are fully understood. The necessary elements of ability to rotate the hips easily, to support the body effortlessly in a small knee bend, to elevate the body rested on ten toes, all allow the body to move as an entire unit — straight down and straight up — a vertical column supported from the earth. When these movements are combined, a bouncing-rubber-ball action results. The jump appears to be executed effortlessly without hoisting through arms, back, shoulders, neck, or head. Breathing remains controlled and unhurried. Practice on a jump board demonstrates the amount of freedom learned in the ability to spring, using all of both feet. The further refinements of programing and sequencing while jumping develop easily through combined bouncing and arm-float matching.

Our prime reason for developing effortless patterns of movement in motor areas in an optometric training program is to build freedoms in those patterns that can be matched with visual patterns for developing solid visualizing skills. We must concurrently develop refinements and build freedoms in the visual sub-skills, preparing them for all other sensory-motor matching.[8]

IN THE SAME manner in which we have developed an awareness in the person of what his body is doing and helped him to understand the difference between the right way and the wrong way of moving in order to correct and refine his move-

---

[6] Milton Fehr, "The Art of Walking," *Prevention Magazine* (December 1958).

[7] M. Feldenkrais, *The Body and Mature Behavior* (New York, N.Y.: International Universities Press, 1966).

[8] C. V. Lyons and Emily B. Lyons, "The Power of Optometric Visual Training: Explored through a Philosophy of Visualization," *Journal of the American Optometric Association* (August 1967). Available in reprint form from the Optometric Extension Program Foundation, Duncan, Oklahoma.

ments, we bring similar understanding of how and what he is doing with his eyes. He must build understanding that the world he sees and comprehends through his eyes is his own special and particular interpretation. His point of view results from information received from two points of view, or two circuits: his right eye and his left eye. If the information received from these two circuits is not in agreement for spatial estimations — such as an object's location, size or clarity — his visual estimations will be inaccurate and distorted. His point of view of himself in relation to the world around him (people, things, situations) will mirror his visual inaccuracies and distortions. He must become aware of these visual differences and learn how to make them compatible. [9]

As he uses the awareness he has learned through body and motor movements, we help him discover that the movements he makes with his eyes are related to and influenced by his body movements. As we use lenses and prisms to change his visual space, he moves through this altered visual field to find that his estimations of his own positioning are dependent on accurate estimations of everything around him. He finds that he is one object among many objects, all interdependent. As he refines and matches motor and visual movements in this way, he grows in the security of how to depend upon and use his total visual field to lead and direct his movements. Refining the use of hands and eyes as a team brings the realization that he can shift to reliance on visual directing for accurate tactile estimations, and that visual directing can equal or surpass what he could do with his hands.

Through fine awareness of many movements through his body, he becomes more sensitive to differentiations of the sounds he speaks and those he hears. He becomes attuned to finding his own mismatches between the qualities of the sound entering his ears and the representation of that sound as he speaks it. He finds that the varying patterns of timing he hears can be accurately matched and produced with his mouth. These refinements in auditory-verbal time sequencing bring increasing freedom and fluency in oral language — the symbolic language from which visual letters and words are built.

To turn identification of visual letters and words into the comprehending, thinking process called "reading" requires a complex matching of time and space movement patterns. The understanding of varying time intervals learned through auditory-verbal means must be related and matched to a similar understanding of space intervals. The learner must find that there is a correlation between the length of time it takes him to say a sound — to stop and start with his voice — and the distance between letters and words. If he accurately matches these varying patterns of time and space, be builds concepts for reading with understanding; if he mismatches these patterns, learning is inaccurate and distorted and information is restricted. [10]

---

[9] Lecture by Bruce R. Wolff at the Northwest Congress of Optometry, Portland, Oregon, December 1958. Transcript is available from the Reporter Company, 2761 S.W. Fairview Boulevard, Portland, Oregon.

[10] C. V. Lyons and Emily B. Lyons, "The Power of Optometric Visual Training as Measured in Factors of Intelligence," *Journal of the American Optometric Association* (December 1954). Available in reprint form from the Optometric Extension Program Foundation, Duncan, Oklahoma.

SENSORY-MOTOR

GAINING freedom and refinement in this highest level of movement pattern — visual symbolic learning — requires understanding in how to hold a thought, an idea, a movement, or a symbol in the mind's eye, free from the necessity of reinforcing visual patterning with other sensory modes, such as tactile or verbal. This does not mean by-passing or dropping out other sensory-motor areas; it merely means finding that visual processing, free of other reinforcement, is the fastest, easiest, and most effortless way to think and to recall.[11]

The further refinement of visualizing — visualization ability — from which productive, innovative, creative thinking develops is not an esoteric something that springs from nowhere into the now; rather, it is a "correlate of activities at various levels."[12] It is the "minutia of minutia" in movement matching, growing from continuing matching and refinements in all systems.[13]

That this is a way of thinking which results from the total action patterns of an individual — a dynamic state of effortlessness — is described well by George I. Brown and Donald Gaynor.[14] They say:

> Creativity has often been regarded as a sedentary or immobile process. A state of calmness, it is assumed, is required, and calmness is generally associated with a minimum of physical action. This, however, seems to be an oversimplification. It is quite likely that an individual in vigorous movement can still be apparently calm. Albert Upton defines this sort of calmness as a state of equilibrium, "equestrian beatitude — Nirvana on horseback" — the stability of a spinning top.[15] The calmness finds its source in what could be described as extreme awareness.

Neurologically or educationally handicapped, learning disabled, average, or superior in potential — whatever the "people" problems and imbalances, freedom to think and create can be expanded. Seeing *with* the eyes and *through* the eyes can be learned, bringing an envelope of freedom to that gravity-bound and restricted creature called Man. From this small island of security we can help him move out to find his own delicately balanced state of mobility. His feet must rest on the earth, but his probing and searching eyes can reach for the stars.

---

[11] C. V. Lyons and Emily B. Lyons, *Visualization Series, Units I and II* (Willits, California: Golden Rule Publications, n.d.).

[12] Edith Meyer, "Comprehension of Spatial Relations in Preschool Children," *Journal of Genetic Psychology*, LVII (1940), 199-151.

[13] A. M. Skeffington, *op. cit.*

[14] George I. Brown and Donald Gaynor, "Athletic Action as Creativity," *Journal of Creative Behavior*, I (Spring 1967).

[15] Albert Upton, *Design for Thinking: A First Book in Semantics* (Palo Alto, Calif.: Stanford University Press, 1961), p. 208.

REFERENCES

Forrest, Elliott B. "Vision and the Language Arts," *Optical Journal Review* (January 15, 1967).

——————. "Man, Movement, and Vision," *The Optometric Weekly* (March 2, March 9, 1967).

Greenstein, Tole. *Visual Development: The Synthesis Approach to Optometric Vision Care and Guidance.* Duncan, Okla.: Optometric Extension Program Foundation, 1966-1967.

Kepes, Gyorgy. *The Nature and Art of Motion.* New York, N.Y.: George Braziller, 1965.

McDonald, Lawrence W. *Visual Training: Series I, II, III.* Duncan, Okla.: Optometric Extension Program Foundation, 1965.

Children are born with their own individual learning mechanisms. It is important to know how they function, to strengthen and modify them in infancy and childhood, and to make use of the child's preferred sense modality when he enters school. There would be no learning-handicapped children if the approaches to learning were flexible enough. However, up to the time the child enters school he has not had a real test of his ability to learn in a formal way. So it may be that not until he enters school will it become apparent that he needs to learn by a method other than that presented for the majority of children his age.

> **— E. Muriel Bennett, M.D.**
> "The Pediatrician's Role in
>   Evaluating the Child with
>   a Learning Disability",
> *Academic Therapy Quarterly,* I
> (Spring 1966).

Visual Perception and Discrimination

Donald W. Hardy
Beverly B. Casebeer

MARK was a child with a consistent history of failure in kindergarten. He seemed shy and uninterested. During games he was certain to be the inattentive child who would become confused and run the wrong way. His ineptitude with scissors, crayons, puzzles, and other standard kindergarten equipment appeared to fall within the performance range of a much younger child. Mark just didn't fit in, and he seemed to be one of those children who just need another year at home to grow up. Routine testing by the guidance department of the Orinda, California, School District, however, indicated that Mark's school problems centered in areas quite different from shyness and immaturity. The Frostig Developmental Test of Visual Perception showed clearly that Mark's problems were related to how he perceived the world around him.[1] Mark was not sent home for another year: he was enrolled in a perceptual-training program which was prepared to meet his individual needs. His perceptual difficulties were carefully diagnosed, and specific teaching strategies were devised on the basis of this diagnosis. Let us turn now to the focal point of this discussion — visual perception and discrimination.

Simply stated, visual perception is the receptive visual input that comes from all of our experiences. Discrimination is the integration of stimuli; it is a process that occurs in the brain. Frostig notes, "In perceiving these four lines ☐ . . . the sensory perception of them occurs in the eye, but the recognition of them as a square occurs in the brain."[2] It is apparent that these functions are vital to such school-centered tasks as learning to read, write, spell, or do arithmetic. G. N. Getman reports the following:

> If you are wondering about this emphasis on vision, recall that children grow up to live in a visual world. Reputable authorities on human behavior now agree and state that vision and intelligence are very closely related. What a child sees and understands, he can know; what a child knows determines his cultural intelligence.[3]

If a child's perceptive facilities are not functioning properly, the whole spectrum of his relationships with his environment will surely be distorted. He cannot

---

[1] Marianne Frostig, *Marianne Frostig Developmental Test of Visual Perception*, (Palo Alto, Calif.: Consulting Psychologists Press, 1961).

[2] Marianne Frostig and David Horne, *The Frostig Program for the Development of Visual Perception* (Chicago, Ill.: Follett, 1964).

[3] G. N. Getman, *How to Develop Your Child's Intelligence* (Luverne, Minn.: The Announcer Press, 1962).

perceive the world as it is, much less respond to it accurately. Whether the perceptual difficulties are a result of minimal brain dysfunction or a developmental lag, they present a critical situation for the classroom teacher. Early diagnosis and remediation are essential. The child must also be seen within the total context of his development, and although in this discussion focus is brought to bear upon specific remedial activities, these teaching strategies must be incorporated within the total educational needs of the child. To state this another way, a child may have difficulties in a number of areas or he may require remediation in one area and be extremely talented or skilled in another. It is suggested that the Marianne Frostig Developmental Test of Visual Perception[4] and The Frostig Program for the Development of Visual Perception[5] are exceptionally useful tools for the identification and remediation of perceptual weaknesses in children. The Frostig program concentrates on five areas: visual-motor skills, perceptual constancy, position in space, spatial relationships, and figure-ground perception. The use of information provided by these instruments should provide the classroom teacher with a means for initiating a program based realistically upon the needs of young children.

The following sections deal specifically with visual perception and discrimination in terms of the subject matter areas of reading, writing, spelling, and arithmetic. A major assumption in each of the subject-matter sections is that the children for whom the lessons are intended are children with visual-perception and discrimination problems. The lessons are specific and practical, and our intention is to present them in developmental form. In other words, the lessons begin with relatively simple or fundamental activities and progress in complexity.

Reading.

A MAJOR TASK confronting the child in visual proficiency is the recognition of likenesses and differences. The child can be taught to recognize such forms as circles, triangles, squares, rectangles, octagons, ovals, and clovers. The forms may be reproduced on ditto or stencil and the child may be asked to draw each shape next to the outline of the shape on his paper (visual recall and motor control). Following this, the child can cut out the forms and paste them on pattern paper. These same forms can be cut into two or three pieces to make puzzles for the child to paste onto the pattern paper. This activity helps the child develop a gestalt for the whole form and later to be able to see the integrated form of these shapes by using them as puzzle pieces. As form perception of simple geometric shapes is developed, the teacher can include recognition of these shapes, using Frostig type figure-ground exercises and perceptual constancy work papers. If the child has worked with a circle by tracing, reproducing, cutting, and pasting it whole and in pieces onto pattern paper, he should also be capable of locating it in a maze of distracting lines (figure-ground recognition). The circle can then be identified in different sizes by "I Spy" games in the classroom. For example, different-sized circles are mixed with other shapes, and the children are asked to "spy" the smallest circle. Finding circles in pictures or objects in the classroom provide variations of this exercise.

---

[4] *Op. Cit.*
[5] *Op. Cit.*

Visual discrimination and motor exercises can be combined in a game where squares, circles, and triangles are placed on the floor and the child may only step on the circles as he wends his way through the maze. By adding music to this activity, the game becomes "Statue," with the children freezing when the needle is lifted from the record. These activities help to establish readiness skills for categorizing and classifying.

As the child becomes increasingly capable of perceiving basic forms, his skill should be extended to the recognition of similar shapes with different inner complexities (patterns). Finer visual awareness can be developed by using complex patterns. Activities of this nature lead into word-analysis studies later on. For example, exercises which require pupils to group circles with stars in them are part of most reading-readiness programs.

AFTER the child has progressed to the point of recognizing inner differences of similar shapes, in addition to whole-form differences, he is ready to extend his activities to object discrimination in pictures. Tasks on the picture level include matching, classifying, and spatial positional relationships (in front of, behind). The following example is given to illustrate instruction on the picture level.

The pupil is shown pictures of a child in front of a chair, in back of a chair, on a chair, and next to a chair. The pupil physically places himself in the various positions shown in the pictures. He has thus, through his own experience, established a basis for being able to relate to what is shown in the picture; he can visually perceive these situations on a picture level. At this point, the child is encouraged to verbalize his experience to provide an added stimulus toward the integration of the learning experience. Pictures of activity scenes are particularly useful in language-development lessons. The child is able to select, reject, and classify according to any category that is appropriate to him. For example, a child who is shown a picture of an outdoor scene might pick out the things that fly, living things, or a certain color. At this point the teacher needs only to supply the visual stimulus and the child will apply perceptual and discrimination skills to perform the task.

By guiding the child to discriminate between the same object with different inner complexities, pictures are utilized to further develop classification skills which were established in earlier lessons. The child is led to observe that a broad category, such as *dog*, can contain any number of subcategories such as *short-tailed, long-eared, short-haired, long-haired*, and so forth. The following activity is suggested for developing this skill.

Place four children with a number of similar physical characteristics in front of the room, and select another child from the class to be "it." The child who is "it" is to pick, as soon as he is able from your clues, the child of whom you are thinking. Suppose you select two blond, blue-eyed girls; one blond, brown-eyed boy. You might then say, "I'm looking at a girl." (This eliminates the boy.) "She has blue eyes." (This eliminates one girl.) The person who is "it" has been able to eliminate two people at this point, but he still has no definitive clue as to which of the remaining girls you are thinking. You might then say, "She is blond." (No clue yet.) "She has two arms." (No clue yet.) "She has a red dress." Now

SENSORY-MOTOR

"it" knows who it is and will terminate the game. While the game is in progress, the remainder of the children in the class will silently play the game too.

Further development of classification skills can be provided by having children work on incomplete pictures to fill in missing parts, having them identify pictures of objects that would normally be found indoors or outdoors, or having them group objects such as rocks and shells into classifications such as rouch, sharp, spotted, and bivalves.

FURTHER development of visual perception and discrimination takes the child into the area of symbols. One activity is to show the child a line and ask him to select a line exactly like it from a series of lines, some of which are shorter or longer, and some of which are in different positions. Beyond this point the developmental lessons include the selection of letters of the alphabet. For example, the child is to select the *b*.

b	d a b q p

This last exercise and others similar to it appear to receive considerable emphasis in kindergarten, and rightly so, considering the developmental level of most kindergarteners. However, when we think of the significant amount of visual-discrimination development which must precede the ability to perform such tasks, it is possible to understand how a child like Mark, and others of his kind, are utterly confounded, frustrated, and frightened when confronted with such exercises. These children must have developmental instruction beginning where they are actually functioning if they are ever to be expected to succeed in our educational system.

After the one-symbol visual discrimination is successfully mastered, the child is ready to approach combinations of letters. In a row of groups of letters, which might include *gab, bga, abg,* and *bag,* he can look for *abg*. This finer visual discrimination leads to the ability to locate such words as *dog* in a row of words which includes *hog, bog, dog,* and *jog*. The child then selects words included in two rows of words. More complex words are introduced, and ultimately three rows of words can be used for discrimination practice. Thus we have a basis for successful reading program.

It is essential that we make note of the fact that visual perception and discrimination do not exist as an autonomous entity. A coordinated effort for the successful development of any skill. The perceptual areas, in turn, must be considered in light of the total developmental requirements of the individual child.

Writing.

SEVERAL EXERCISES are appropriate for the strengthening of visual perception in writing. Worksheets with circles on them provide the child with the opportunity for tracing. Worksheets with lines from left to right on the page can also be used. Tracing between two lines without touching either and tracing lines that cross over each other without losing the figure-ground pattern of either line are both useful activities. As the child becomes increasingly proficient, he should be able to trace overlapping circles, stars, squares, and triangles without losing the figure-ground relationship. He can then color pictures where different parts have different colors. This particular skill provides an example of the differences between a child who is visually immature and one who is not. A visually immature child will color an entire picture one color without seeing the parts or recognizing that parts of the picture should be different in color. As visual discrimination develops, the child will stop as he comes to a section where a change of color is appropriate and will make the change. The teacher can assist in the development of this skill by encouraging the child to outline the area he wishes to color, thus setting limits for himself.

At this point the child is ready to trace letters and numbers. He should also be given the opportunity to color-in fat letters and numbers as well as to color around letters and numbers without going into the form. In this manner the visual awareness of boundaries and form in writing is developed.

The following activities are more advanced in difficulty. The child traces letters that are the same size, then he traces letters that are the same shape. For example, the letter *h* might be in a row including *n, g, h,* and *l*. The child traces only the *h*. This activity progresses to the point where the child will eventually be confronted with a row that includes all *h*'s except for one *n*. He should trace all the *h*'s. As this writing skill is developed the teacher should stress the letter name. Further development in writing is carried out with the child finishing incomplete letters and finally forming letters of his own.

At this juncture, the child is ready to copy from the board to his paper — in other words, far point to near point. He looks at visual shapes on the chalkboard and reproduces them on his paper. Visual memory is strengthened by the teacher flashing a shape and then asking the child to reproduce the shape after a time lapse of approximately five seconds.

A child who is neurologically handicapped may have difficulty visualizing some of the forms he is to reproduce. In this case, extensive chalkboard reproduction involving kinesthetic, tactile, experience activities may be necessary. It is considered particularly important that children with visual-perceptual disorders be engaged in a motor-development program which coordinates his inner awareness with his expressive skills. Walking-board activities, jumping-board routines, and movement-exploration activities are all part of a good visual perception and discrimination program. The Kephart activities, for example, have been used with considerable success to help children like Mark.[6]

Spelling.

THE SPELLING PROGRAM begins with visual-auditory discrimination activities. Since this skill involves more than just gestalt recognition of words, the child needs to develop words from their parts. Handwriting appears to be of prime importance in the development of spelling ability. The gestalt of the word cannot emerge when lack of motor control causes the configuration to be distorted — in other words, when handwriting is poor. Many of us, after having

---

[6] Newell C. Kephart and D. H. Radler, *Success Through Play* (New York, N.Y.: Harper and Row, 1960).

written a word poorly, have had the sensation that a word doesn't look right even though we have spelled it correctly.

The teacher should present strong auditory stimulation in the spelling program. As the child sees individual likenesses and differences in words, he should also hear those likenesses and differences. For example, a spelling word might be presented as follows. The child looks at a word as the teacher carefully pronounces it for him. He points at what he can hear in the word as the teacher pronounces it, they discuss each letter of the word separately, and the teacher and child then spell the word together. Next, the child traces the word in the air and then on his desk while spelling it out loud. He closes his eyes and traces the word on his paper. (At this point the child is integrating the word.) Finally, the child writes the word and reads it from his own handwriting. The child should then use the word in a sentence in order to see it in context with other words. This approach to spelling begins with individual letters, progresses to words, and finally to sentences.

Teaching families of words is a helpful device for working with children with learning problems. For example, the child having difficulty with word synthesis can usually master a sequence of words such as *like, bike, hike, Mike, dike,* and *pike.*

Arithmetic.

THE SCOPE of the arithmetic program extends from the concrete-objects level to the picture level, and finally moves to the symbolic level. To develop skill in number recognition, the child begins with one object and one number. If the child has difficulty visualizing quantity in relation to symbols, he will need experiences visualizing and manipulating concrete objects. He needs to practice writing numbers in their correct order, with visual concentration on their sequence. For example, the number *twenty-one* must be written *21,* not *12.* This practice may be extended through ones, tens, and hundreds. Math concepts can be further extended by activities that require the child to visualize *more, less, longer, shorter, equal, plus, minus, mass, space, form,* and *order.* Pegboards, chalkboard pictures, stacking materials, three-dimensional forms, and take-apart materials are useful in the development of math concepts. The child who can visually make simple, adjacent, and interlocking forms on a pegboard is able to deal with forms as a whole. If he can successfully relate two lines on a chalkboard as being equal, longer, or shorter, he is able to visualize a necessary math concept. If he can erase part of a line to make it equal to another, he has performed the process of subtraction. If he can stack blocks and see that one stack is more than another, he is adding. If he can successfully take apart a manipulative device, he is capable of understanding division. If he can construct a three-dimensional block building, he is dealing successfully with spatial relationships. The child who can visualize spatial relationships and positions of objects in space can conceptualize numbers and number values through his integration of experience and visual memory.

Many neurologically handicapped children have poor ocular control. The teacher is usually able to recognize this kind of difficulty while the child is pursuing some of the more demanding visual tasks, such as reading or writing.

One exercise requires the child to hold his head still and respond to teacher directions to look *up, down, left, right,* and so forth. The child can also visually track a line on the chalkboard in a controlled direction.[7]

THIS DISCUSSION has been intended to provide the reader with concrete examples of classroom instruction in reading, writing, spelling, and arithmetic, with focus on the development of visual perception and discrimination. Each instructional program for each child, however, must be uniquely suited to that child's particular needs, and the difficult burden of matching learning experiences to the needs of pupils rests ultimately with the classroom teacher. It is hoped that the information presented here will in some small way be of assistance to teachers in accomplishing that goal.

REFERENCES

Beck, Joan. "Unlocking the Secrets of the Brain," *Chicago Tribune Magazine*, September 13 and September 27, 1964.

Clements, Sam D. *Some Aspects of the Characteristics, Management, and Education of the Child with Minimal Brain Dysfunction.* Little Rock, Ark.: Arkansas Association for Children with Learning Disabilities, 1966.

Cruckshank, William M., et al. *A Method for Brain-Injured and Hyperactive Children.* Syracuse, N.Y.: Syracuse University Press, 1961.

Dolch, Edward William. *Helping Handicapped Children in School.* Champaign, Ill.: Garrard Press, 1948.

Fernald, Grace M. *Remedial Techniques in Basic School Subjects.* New York, N.Y.: McGraw-Hill, 1943.

Gesell, Arnold, and Frances L. Ilg. *Infant and Child in the Culture of Today.* New York, N.Y.: Harper and Brothers, 1943.

Glasser, William. *Reality Therapy.* New York, N.Y.: Harper and Row, 1965.

Hackett, Layne C., and Robert G. Jensen. *A Guide to Movement Exploration.* Palo Alto, Calif.: Peek Publications, 1966.

Kephart, Newell C. *The Slow Learner in the Classroom.* Columbus, Ohio: Charles E. Merrill, 1960.

Kirk, Samuel A. *Educating Exceptional Children.* Boston, Mass.: Houghton Mifflin, 1962.

McGinnis, Mildred A. *Aphasic Children.* Washington, D.C.: Alexander Graham Bell Association for the Deaf, 1963.

Montessori, Maria. *Dr. Montessori's Own Handbook.* New York, N.Y.: Schocken Books, 1965.

Orton, Samuel Torrey. *Reading, Writing, and Speech Problems in Children.* New York, N.Y.: W. W. Norton, 1937.

Roucek, Joseph S. (ed.) *The Difficult Child.* New York, N.Y.: Philosophical Library, 1964.

Spraings, Violet E. (instructor). "Perceptual, Perceptual-Motor, and Learning Disabilities of the Educationally Handicapped." A course offered by the University of California, Berkeley, summer 1968.

---

[7] For a discussion of this topic, see Kephart and Radler, *ibid.*

Tuning In

Martha Serio
Jane Faelchle

NEUROLOGICALLY impaired children are easily the most misunderstood, the most disliked, and the most misjudged group in our classrooms. When expected to compete in large classes with children whose sensory-motor systems are intact, they are misfits. When the records of a small group of these children who had auditory problems were scanned, the following remarks, made by their former classroom teachers, were disclosed.

Will not pay attention.
Slow to respond to verbal questions.
Cries easily.
Work habits poor.
Has achieved nothing.
Immature and restless.
Inconsistent performance.
Evades questions when he doesn't feel like answering them.
Expresses himself poorly.
Stubborn and uncooperative in class.
Mentally retarded and should be excluded from school.
Withdrawn and oblivious to objects and people around him.
Not "tuned in" to the classroom activities.

In most school systems the weight of the responsibility for recognizing and seeking help and resources for the proper placement of these children rests with the classroom teachers and administrators. Every educator needs certain basic knowledge about learning disorders and their causes, and they must become aware of the need for early detection and identification if these children are to make a successful adjustment.

The procedures and materials to be used in this program are important, but they must not be regarded as methods in themselves. Materials are but one means of reaching these children, and within limits, the amount and kind of materials will depend upon the teacher and the type of problems that require her aid. Materials are used to demonstrate or to integrate a process. With patience and the right procedures and materials, children with auditory problems can be taught, and definite improvement can be achieved in their total learning capacity.

The approach to remediation is important in the instruction of children who have learning disorders due to neurological dysfunctions. These children have developmental gaps and a general unevenness in learning because their impairment often distorts or permits only small portions of information to filter through. A program that is effective, and one that is optimistic in its scope, is one that utilizes an approach of readiness and remediation in all areas of the child's educational program. This type of program is based on the premise that, in any learning situation, further unevenness in learning can be prevented by helping the child to sequentially build generalizations and concepts. It also helps in finding where the gaps exist in order to plan measures of remediation.

Alfred A. Strauss and Newell C. Kephart have devised a program of this type which we have found to be most helpful and adaptable.[1] This program employs sequential steps in the development and building of generalizations. These steps are as follows:

- Gradients.
- Differences.
- Likenesses.
- Contour, shape, and form.
- Integration of sense fields.
- Spatial relationships.
- Language and vicarious experiences.
- Concepts.

These steps will be referred to frequently in the following discussion of educational procedures and materials which are helpful in educating children who have problems in managing auditory information.

AUDITORY PERCEPTION

WHAT are the problems most frequently exhibited by children who have auditory impairments? Why do they behave as they do in the classrooms? There are three basic ways in which learning may be impeded neurologically. Although the child may have no loss in the sensory function, as do the blind and the deaf, the neurologically impaired child has a reduced ability in using his sensory areas effectively. The detriment may be in the receptive (input), expressive (output), or the integrative functions and may involve the verbal or nonverbal areas.

Disturbances of the auditory channel affect perception and behavior, and it is of the utmost importance that they be detected. Auditory receptive abilities may be affected in many ways. If the deficiencies are found to be at the level of perception, the sounds in the environment are bewildering to the child, and he

---

[1] Alfred A. Strauss and Newell C. Kephart, *Psychopathology and Education of the Brain-Injured Child, Vol. II* (New York, N.Y.: Grune and Stratton, 1955), pp. 47-53.

will have difficulty selecting or even attending to relevant and purposeful sounds. He will misperceive what he hears. Comprehension is limited, for sounds cannot be discriminated in words that sound alike. This detriment further impedes the ability to blend sounds into words, as well as the ability to divide words into syllables. Blending and syllabication abilities are important in learning to read effectively.

Memory span is often deficient in children with learning disabilities. Either the span or the sequence involved in the repetition of a number of digits or words in sentences may be found to be faulty, affecting the material as a whole as it is received by the child.

The expression, or output, area reflects the child's perceptual development. When he expresses himself, the quantity and quality of his receptive language is revealed. His language will show his ability to remember words, sequences, syntactical structures, and it will reveal any speech difficulties caused by faulty discrimination. This relationship between receptive and expressive processes must not be overlooked in the diagnosis and remediation of a child's difficulties.

Expression may be deficient while the reception is basically intact, and conversely, reception can be basically intact with the expression areas intact. Difficulties in the output may affect both verbal and nonverbal functions. Memory for what one wishes to say and the motor system for expression reveal the interaction between these systems, and the defect may be in the association process. To speak requires the ability to recall and remember words, but it also requires the ability to relate these messages to the appropriate motor systems.

It is important to the discussion of expressive disorders to observe the difficulty these children have in generalizing and categorizing. They often have difficulty with multiple-word meanings, appearing rigid in thought and concept formation. It appears that any brain disruption that may interfere or modify learning may interfere with the ability to conceptualize.

Children with auditory difficulties have problems with the more subtle and complex problems in the nonverbal areas. In the development of language, it is necessary to relate words to nonverbal experience. Deficiencies in nonverbal learning demonstrate the inability to estimate or recall time (seasons, months, weeks, days, hours). Likewise, the measurement of distance, size, volume, shape, height, and weight present difficulties for these youngsters. These concepts involve the quantitative aspects of experience, such as *fast* and *slow, far* and *near, large* and *small, tall* and *short, high* and *low.*

The preceding discussion, necessarily oversimplified, indicates that various aspects of learning can be involved with many combinations of the input and output, verbal and nonverbal areas being affected, making it necessary to employ differential diagnosis and specific educational procedures. It is difficult to diagnose the many problems of these children because of the many involvements. It is important, however, to delineate the child's strengths and weaknesses in all areas in order that a suitable remedial and readiness program may be planned. It bears repetition that the best results are realized if diagnosis is made and remediation started at the earliest age possible.

Before discussing an educational program and activities for children with generalized deficiency in auditory learning, it is significant to restate the objective: We must help these children to utilize all their capabilities. A multisensory approach in the readiness and remediation program should be used as a means of stimulating all possible areas of learning. We should, however, be constantly aware of the possibility of "overloading." Helmer Myklebust says:

> The multisensory approach, if used promiscuously, can be damaging. A child may deal effectively with information involving intraneurosensory processes but show symptoms of disintegration when interneurosensory and complex integrative functions are required.[2]

Such signs of disintegration are revealed by random movements, poor attention, poor recall, confusion, and disinhibitions.

AUDITORY DISCRIMINATION

THE INITIAL STAGE in educating children with auditory disabilities begins with the awareness and discrimination of sound. Auditory training should be an integral part of the total education of these children, and every effort should be made to remediate or develop auditory perception involving the areas of awareness, localization, sequentialization, and memory of sound. These children need to structure their auditory world, sorting out and associating sounds with specific experiences or objects. These activities should be arranged in sequential steps, from the reception of gross sounds to activities involving the finer and more subtle use of sounds in syllables, words, and sentences. Although activities in auditory discrimination are numerous, I will mention only a few here as examples.

Awareness of sound.

Using a bell, a horn, a rattle, and finally the voice, the teacher has the child perform a specific act while the sound is occurring. For example, she might have him raise his hand, stand up, or walk. He stops the activity when the sound stops.

Another activity which can be used to good advantage with a small group is to pass a ball around a circle of children while a phonograph record is played, stopping when the music stops. This activity is particularly good because the amplification can be controlled and changed.

Activities involving sounds of the environment should be included because the children must be made aware of them so that they can learn to relate to them. Records or tapes of different categories of sound experiences can be purchased, or even better, they can be made by the teacher. These sounds might include outdoor sounds, classroom sounds, city sounds, farm sounds, zoo sounds, etc. It is also helpful to display pictures that are matched to the environmental sounds heard on the tape or record.[3]

Finer assessments of sound can be made by using Montessori sound boxes. The teacher can make these boxes by filling milk cartons with material — putting

---

[2] Doris Johnson and Helmer Myklebust, *Learning Disabilities* (New York, N.Y.: Grune and Stratton, 1967), p. 31.

[3] An excellent collection of recorded sounds and related pictures may be found in *Sounds I Can Hear* (Oakland, N.Y.: Scott Foresman, 1966).

the same material, such as rice, sugar, pennies, seeds, marbles, stones, etc., in each of two cartons. The children are then asked to match up the two cartons having the same sound.

When the child is able to make the above sound discriminations, he is ready to use the more difficult sound components that make up our speech. Teachers are familiar with the simple activities of matching various sounds of letters (*b, c, bl, d*) to pictures of objects which start with these sounds *(ball, cake, block, doll.)* It is important to the child's introduction to reading that he participate successfully in this activity. For this reason, many variations should be introduced. One can keep the child motivated by using a flannel board, boxes, envelopes, or baskets.

At this level, use can be made of the numbers, sounds, and words the child uses and needs to identify accurately. The child can circle or mark numbers and words in response to oral dictation by the teacher or to a tape recorder. There are many lists of similar-sounding words that are excellent to use for auditory-discrimination exercises.

Another discrimination activity at this level is to use a series of sentence pictures in which two words are interchanged. For example:

The girl is running.
The girl is jumping.
The boy is running.
The baby is running.
The man is running.

The discrimination of one sound versus many sounds is one method of working with the figure-ground of sound. A child should be able to pick out a specific sound among others and to attend to this sound only. Using the tape of the outdoor sound experiences mentioned earlier, the child listens for the sound of an airplane, a car, or a bird and indicates when he hears that particular sound (among other sounds) and how long he can hear it.

Many of these activities may be repeated with the addition of a noise in the background, such as low-volume phonograph or radio music, with the child being directed to concentrate on the activity, learning to exclude extraneous sounds.

Comparison of sounds.

THE INITIAL STAGE of comparing sounds can start with using the sounds of a bicycle horn, a drum, a whistle, and a bell. These sounds could be catagorized as loud and soft sounds. This comparison of sounds could be further developed by the teacher initiating a loud or soft drumbeat and the child imitating it. Pitch discrimination, using a piano or a xylophone, is helpful in teaching a child to distinguish between high- and low-pitched sounds. Some children need practice to learn to imitate a high or low pitch.

Discrimination of fast and slow sounds also may be initiated with the beat of a drum. The child responds by walking or running to the tempo of the drumbeat. A series of phonograph records can be used, each varying distinctly in rhythm: marching, skipping, running, walking, and leaping.

Next in this area of comparing sounds is the development of rhyming sounds in words. Here again, there are many commercial materials and games available to the teacher. Because of the difficulty children with auditory disabilities have with rhyming, care should be taken to follow sequential steps. Isolated rhyming words should be used first, and later rhyming phrases should be introduced. Finally, the words that rhyme in poems should be analyzed.

Localization of sound.

The child with an auditory involvement may have difficulty locating sounds. He must learn to do this in order to react appropriately to the sound. For a beginning, one activity is to blindfold the child and seat him in the center of the room. The child is instructed to point to the place from which he thinks the teacher is ringing a bell, hitting a drum, or talking. The teacher might stand in the following positions in relation to the child: front, right front, right side, left side, left front, above left front, above right front, and the corresponding positions in the rear of the child.

Children who experience difficulty with auditory focus may be helped by learning to locate sounds in words at the initial, medial, or final position (*chi*cken, ki*tch*en, ca*tch*). A similar activity using numerals in a series might also be used (2573, 34213, 7342).

To develop the ability to localize particular sounds, phrases that include a key word in various positions can be used. For example, using the word *in* as the key word, the following phrases might be introduced: *in* the house; come *in*; come *in* and see; *in* the tree; and walk *in*.

Auditory memory and sequentialization.

Auditory memory, remembering a sequence of sounds within words and a sequence of words within sentences, is important for developing the ability to comprehend and use language effectively. One exercise that is helpful in this area is for the child to listen as the teacher bounces a ball or drops beads into a can. The child is then asked to imitate the activity.

Moving on to speech and language, a child is asked to repeat simple phrases such as the following:

Go in.

Go on.

Go up.

Do go on.

I do go.

Is it so?

Is he to go?

I am to go.

As the child progresses, the number of words to be remembered in sequence should be increased:

He can go too.

I can go to you.

He can go by me.

Activities in which the child is asked to follow a series of directions, working from the simple to the complex, are also helpful in developing sequentialization and memory. For example:

Stand up.

Stand up and hop on your right foot.

Stand up, hop around your chair, and put both hands on your head.

Another method for ascertaining a child's auditory memory is to read a short paragraph and have the child recount the facts, the sequence of events, the names of the characters, etc.

The Peabody Language Development Kits contain many kinds of activities for developing the skills of sequentialization, rhyming, and auditory memory.[4] These kits may be used as a resource and a guide for planning remedial programs for individual children or for a group of children.

Whenever possible, these auditory lessons should be followed by a visual activity — work with pencil and paper or at the chalkboard — that is related to the experience. This follow-up is necessary in order to reinforce learning.

THE THREE R'S

VARIOUS TYPES of auditory disturbances interfere with the ability to read. The teacher needs to observe a child's capacity to hear similarities and differences in words, to follow auditory sequence and direction, to blend sounds into words, and to change word wholes into syllables and individual sounds.

Mistakes are important in this classroom. Teachers must cultivate a listening ear and a note-taking hand and listen to children in their activities. For example, a checklist in oral reading should include the following: the number and type of word-recognition difficulties, including omissions, substitutions, reversal errors, inability to use context clues, actual mispronunciations; the ability to read by phrases, to use punctuation; the ability to comprehend and recall the material read. General observations of the child's reading behavior should also be noted, *i.e.* finger-pointing, voice quality and control, head movements, and any signs of developing frustration. Likewise, a similar checklist should be kept when working with a child in arithmetic and in written- and oral-language activities. This is one method of analyzing the child's deficits, and his mistakes are an indication of and a key to the program to be used with that particular child.

Children with auditory involvement respond best to a whole-word approach during the initial stages of reading instruction. Since their problems are in auditory perception, memory, and integration, they will be unable to use phonic skills until after they have developed a sight vocabulary. Their work will proceed from the whole word to the analysis of the parts that make up a word.

Because these children have language problems, beginning reading should include what the child sees, hears, and can say. Having the children write words

---

[4] Lloyd M. Dunn and James O. Smith (eds.), *The Peabody Language Kits* (Circle Pines, Minn.: American Guidance Service, 1966).

related to their own experiences proves to be successful and interesting. Particular care should be taken, however, to use words that are different in both auditory and visual configuration so that they can be identified easily.

Writing can reinforce beginning reading, since there is a relationship between reading and writing; both are forms of the spoken word. Writing helps the child to see the separate letters that make up the whole word as well as to think of the sounds they represent. As a child records a word, he must think of the sequence of sounds and the patterns that are perceived visually. Copying words from his reading book and using these words in short sentences is more beneficial for the child than dittoed, unrelated exercises such as, "Mark the letter that is different: d, d, b; s, a, s; p, p, g."

In arithmetic, some children with auditory problems have little trouble with understanding quantitative relationships but do have difficulty understanding the words used to describe processes and understanding word meanings in story problems. They may have little difficulty with computation but have more difficulty with reasoning and vocabulary.

The lack of vocabulary and language is the real problem which impedes learning for these children, whether it is learning to multiply in arithmetic or reading a story filled with many ambiguities and multiple-word meanings. When presenting new processes in mathematics and new concepts in reading, the experience should begin at the most concrete level, reducing the task to a level these children can understand. It is helpful to use concrete materials and life-like experiences, allowing the child to learn to handle these before introducing difficult abstract symbols.

The concept of time is difficult for children with auditory problems to understand. Too many times it is introduced on the twenty-third day because it is on page twenty-three in the arithmetic workbook. These children will learn the concept associated with time quicker and with more ease when they have a need to use it. I remember one day when time was important to both the teacher and the children, and the learning experience that evolved was both interesting and valuable. The problem arose on a Friday when "indoor recess" followed four days of rain. This was not a pleasant situation — forty neurologically impaired children in one classroom. One disgruntled little boy asked the equally disgruntled teacher, "Do I have to rest more than I have to play?" This suggested a different activity. When the children were assembled, the little boy's question was discussed, and this led to an investigation about clocks and time. What shapes are most clocks? What do we call the part of the clock that has the numbers? Could a big clock be made out of children? How many children would we need? Where would these twelve children stand? How many marks are on the clock between each number? Could we take five steps between each of our "numbers"? How many steps does it take to go around the entire clock? What are these steps called when we tell time?

The teacher continued to ask questions in order to guide the children into the discovery of the concepts necessary to tell time. What fun everyone had — particularly the boy whose question originated the activity. He was happy to discover that he rested for only thirty minutes each day, while he was allowed to play for forty minutes.

Arithmetic can be related to almost every subject in the curriculum. It should not be treated as an isolated subject. Science and social studies are rich in the concepts of time and sequence, such as the study of seasons and the calendar. Physical-education activities abound with mathematical concepts of *how many* and *how far*.

IT IS IMPORTANT for the teachers of these neurologically impaired children to teach in the sequence of perceptual steps necessary to reach the higher intellectual skills. The sequence starts with sensation; it proceeds through perception, imagery, and symbolization; and it moves finally to conceptualization. Experiences should be categorized on the basis of concept development rather than being subject-centered.

Each new concept must be made concrete, and it should be presented, whenever possible, by direct experience, or it should be experienced vicariously through films, film strips, recordings, photographs, books, discussions, or even by "acting out." Such experiences will help the child to come into contact with the problem at hand and to relate to it. Learnings must be in the areas of vocabulary, classification, and generalizations. These children need to bake cookies, make lemonade, go for walks to observe the changes in their environment, see and touch different animals, and take trips to the store to buy something they need. These experiences will help them to "tune in" to the world around them with the result that they will begin to learn to the best of their abilities.

The development of self-esteem is the major task of those who presume to guide the young. Anything which prevents its development is de-humanizing and can only lead the young away from the human family and prevent them from enjoying that which is human: To love and to be loved, to have a sense of the future and a feeling of continuity with the past, to have some control over their own destiny and to know that to do this they must *acquire and transmit knowledge and skills.* Without self-esteem, they cannot enjoy the human condition.

— **Floria Coon-Teters**
"Human Considerations in the Education of
  Educationally Handicapped Adolescents,"
Academic Therapy, IV
(Spring 1969)

A Map in the Head

Jack Wahl

A LOOK around a room should organize the room for a child. If his perception is incomplete, if he is attracted to one bright object and then another without any order, a jigsaw puzzle rather than a map results in his mind. His world is made up of fragments which are unconnected and unrelated. This child must learn to organize his looking in order to see everything in the room as related.

Any adult who has ever moved to an unfamiliar town has some idea of this kind of fragmentation. The new arrival moves into a house and goes to work. At first, as far as his perception of his surroundings is concerned, the town exists only as the path from house to work. Over a period of time, the shopping center, downtown, schools, parks, etc., become part of the internal map of the town he carries with him. After several months, he may find that the trip from his house to work could be made much shorter by taking another route. Because a connected, related internal map exists, a shortcut can be "seen." For example, I know of a college student who drove completely around a lake, a distance of over two miles, to get to a freeway that was three blocks from her starting point but in the opposite direction from the way she went. It was not until she was showing her family the campus and surrounding area that she happened to take the shorter route and discovered what she had been doing. This student did not have a good sense of direction and had not realized that she was going almost completely around the lake (in a circle). Some children are as lost in a room as this student was lost in a strange city.

This article will attempt to present a series of conducted tours of some common areas that some children seem unable to organize for themselves.

To test this ability to see relationships, I have a student draw the objects (tables, pictures, chairs, etc.) which are against the wall opposite him. This Wahl Map Test has no norms, but it is easy to recognize special disorientation in the maps drawn of any convenient wall. Figures 1 and 2 are maps of the same wall drawn by students of the same age (eight years, eleven months). Three pictures were hung on the wall approximately as shown in Figure 1. The student who drew Figure 2 bunched them all together so that they were not properly arranged in relation to the couch. Although a sophisticated reader will recognize other per-

SENSORY-MOTOR

Figure 1.

Figure 2.

ceptual distortions in Figure 2, this lack of ability to relate objects — in this case the couch and the pictures — is the inability with which this article is concerned.[1]

In teaching a child to see relationships, the best reference point with which to start is the child himself. For a child to see himself as the center of the universe is not only acceptable, but necessary. Therefore, a good place to start teaching space relations is with the student's hands. Have the student sit with both hands on the table, fists closed, but with thumbs sticking up. Have the student look from one thumb to the other, starting with the thumbs two or three inches apart. Watch the student's eyes to see if they look rapidly from one thumb to the other without going too far and coming back or looking away and then back. When the thumbs are over a foot apart, any student will have trouble getting his eyes from one thumb to the other, so ten to twelve inches should be the maximum space between the thumbs.[2]

If the student's eyes jump erratically around until they happen to land on the thumb, give him a ball to roll from one hand to the other. Have him keep his eyes on the ball. Don't let him roll it fast or move his hands too far apart. The idea is to give the child a visual crutch to help him find his other hand. With some students, it is necessary to place the ball in a trough (a piece of molding or the center tube from a roll of paper towels cut in half lengthways works well). Have the child grasp each end of the trough and tip it, rolling the ball back and forth. Having the student raise his thumbs as the ball touches his hands helps relate the visual and kinesthetic clues.

After the student is able to look from one thumb to the other when they are a foot apart, put a piece of cardboard in front of his eyes and have him put his dominant hand on the table with his thumb up. He should be able to "look through" the cardboard to where his thumb is. A good way to test his ability to perform this task is to give him a card with a word or letter printed on it and have him hold the card. Move aside the cardboard that is in front of the child's eyes and then move it immediately back into place. Ask the child what was on the card. If he knows where his hand is, he will have been looking at it and will have seen the word on the card. Some children have such poor kinesthetic feedback that they can never succeed at this task. It is worth trying as a method of diagnosis, if nothing else. I question the value of kinesthetic teaching methods for a child who is unable to learn this exercise.

---

[1] For those who wish to use a more structured means of evaluation, the following tests are recommended: K. E. Beery, *Developmental Test of Visual-Motor Integration* (Chicago, Ill.: Follett, 1967); G. B. Fuller and J. Laird, "The Minnesota Percepto-Diagnostic Test," *Journal of Clinical Psychology*, XVI (1963), 1-33; E. M. Koppitz, *The Bender Gestalt Test for Children* (New York, N.Y.: Grune and Stratton, 1964); Violet Spraings, *The Spraings Multiple-Choice Bender Gestalt Test* (Olympia, Wash.: Sherwood Press, 1966).

[2] J. Hyde, "Some Characteristics of Voluntary Human Ocular Movements in the Horizontal Plane," *American Journal of Opthamology*, XLVIII (1959), 84-94.

SENSORY-MOTOR

THE NEXT STOP in the child's conducted tour of his visual world uses a ball hung from the ceiling by a string. The student swings the ball from one hand to the other and initially sits so that the ball hangs between his hands. As he succeeds in following the ball — as determined by the teacher watching his eyes as they move — he can engage in fancy swinging, throwing the ball out and back, etc. If the teacher sits in front of the student in a way that allows the ball to swing over his own head, he will be able to watch the student's eyes diverge and converge as the ball swings near and then retreats. When the student can keep track of the ball as he controls it, he is ready for the next step. This is a form of catch, with the teacher catching the ball and swinging it back. At this point, the child must know where the teacher is in the room. The student must swing the ball to the teacher, not just at him. For variation, the student can swing the ball to the ceiling or to the walls. The task here is to have the ball touch the ceiling or the wall, but not bang against it. A little of this variation is all that should be attempted at one time, since it is a difficult task and the student may ask the teacher to demonstrate how it is done — a request that usually leads to a lot of laughs but no success.

When the student swings the ball to the teacher, the teacher should catch it and move his arm in or out from his body so that the ball does not return to the student from exactly the same angle each time. If the teacher is working with directionality and the names for right and left, these can be introduced here by having the student swing the ball to one side or the other of the teacher. The student should tell the teacher which side of his own body the ball comes to when it is returned. Patting the ball back and forth, alternating hands each time, helps the student develop his sense of directionality and space at the same time. Patting it just hard enough to reach the teacher with one hand and then the other requires knowledge of the relative strengths of each side of the body as they relate to the distance the teacher is from the student.

When the student and teacher have exhausted the variations possible with the ball hanging from the ceiling, they can play catch. It is helpful to bounce the ball back and forth rather than to throw it. It requires more attention to distance to bounce a ball once and have it arrive at the other person at the top of the second bounce than merely to throw the ball. At first it may be necessary to put a mark on the floor and have the student aim at it. Later, the student should be able to look at the teacher and still have the ball hit at approximately the same place on the floor each time it is thrown.

As soon as the student can "bounce to," two balls should be used, with the student and teacher each throwing at the same time. The student must now shift his attention from the ball he is throwing to the ball that is being bounced to him. When he is able to work with the teacher so well that the thrown balls hit each other as they hit the floor, he has more than enough control — unless the teacher cannot hit the same place each time, of course!

THE STUDENT now has made the transition from knowing where something is because he is touching it to knowing where it is by looking at it. The next step is to relate the things he sees to each other. The student is given one small flashlight while the teacher uses another. The room is darkened, but not so much that the student cannot see everything in the room clearly. The teacher then shines his flashlight on one wall of the room. The student's and the teacher's light should make a single spot on the wall. The teacher then slowly moves his light while the student tries to keep his light aimed at the teacher's. When the student can move his light with some proficiency, the teacher gets "tricky" by shining his light on the edge of something the student cannot see because of the differences in the position of teacher and student — for example, the side of a desk. It is helpful to let the student work out this problem for himself. If he doesn't succeed the first time, the teacher should continue, moving his light somewhere where the student can again see it. The goal is to have the student realize that he cannot see everything in the room from where he is, and that someone else in the room can see things he cannot. Letting the student lead and the teacher follow with his light sometimes helps the student to arrive at this realization.

If a student is more kinesthetically oriented — if he had no trouble looking "through" the cardboard at his thumb — he may learn faster by having the flashlight strapped to his head as if it were a miner's lamp. To follow the teacher's light under these circumstances, the student must move his head.

When the objects in the room have become familiar to the student through having them emphasized by a light, the student is asked to draw a map of the room from memory. If he succeeds, he can then be asked to look around another room without the help of the teacher's light, and then draw a map of the new room from memory. (The map-drawing procedure is the same whether the flashlight is in the student's hand or strapped to his head.)

The final step is to blindfold the student and have him point to various things in the room. Each time he points to an object, he should be allowed to look in order to reinforce his correct response or to correct his inaccurate response. In the classroom, having the students draw maps of the places they have been — even of the school — reinforces the desire to relate things in the environment to each other.

In simple addition and multiplication, order is not important ($2+3=3+2$), so a lack of spacial orientation can be hidden. When subtraction is introduced, the organization of the problem becomes very important.

Often a student will read 4-3 as four subtracted from three. He may simply have the terminology mixed up, but sometimes his confused spacial organization leads him to make a rule: "The difference between the two numbers is the answer," which leads to $23-17=14$. This student reasons that the difference between 7 and 3 is 4, and the difference between 20 and 10 is 10; therefore, the answer is 14. If possible, the spacially disoriented student should not be taught subtraction until he can do two-place addition, and then subtraction should be introduced immediately with some two-place problems so that a wrong rule will not be learned.

Something as simple as isolating each problem by drawing a box around it creates a restricted area that can be organized by the student. Even more extreme, one might put one problem on each sheet of paper. Within the box, the child can learn that the number on the bottom (or to the right) is taken from the number at the top (or to the left.)

SENSORY-MOTOR

THE SAME PRINCIPLE of restrictive complexity can be applied in spelling. The order of letters in one word can be learned by having the student see only the letters that make up that word. At first, the student should be given the letters and told the word he should spell. Later he can try to recall the letters and the order. He should be told when he has all of the right letters but has them in the wrong order.

Many kinesthetic students (the ones that can look at their thumb when it is behind the cardboard) organize words by writing them. They copy every word they do not recognize and often recognize it as soon as they have copied it. For these students, writing the words on different surfaces (paper, chalkboard, etc.) and in different sizes (as small as they can and as big as they can) seems to be the best place to start a conducted tour of their environment.

A few other ideas for teaching the spatially disoriented child are as follows:

In my studio, I have a chalkboard that is eight feet high and eight feet wide. I often have a student use the entire chalkboard to write one word. Relating the formation of the letters to extreme gross muscle activity helps him to remember the organization of the word. Students who are spatially disoriented are also helped by manipulatable words such as are found in *The Rolling Reader* and Gattegno's *Teaching Reading with Words in Color*.[3] Being able to move words around until they make sense helps these children to learn the importance of the order of words.

The student who cannot see the way things are related to each other in space is probably the same student who cannot recall the proper sequence of letters when he tries to write a word, who cannot keep the sequence of the story he tries to tell you, and who cannot understand why 832 divided by 8 cannot be 14. The teacher can either try to put each part of this student's world together or to put the whole thing together. It is my suggestion that you at least *try* the whole world first.

---

[3] B. H. Stolpen, *Linguistic Block Series* (Chicago, Ill.: Scott Foresman, 1963); C. Gattegno, *Teaching Reading with Words in Color* (New York, N.Y.: Xerox Corporation, (1968).

Arithmetic and Language Skills Developed Through Emphasis on Counting Sequences

Florence A. Sharp

MATHEMATICAL ability has been considered the highest mental functioning—"pure reasoning." We now know, however, that adequate perceptual-motor functioning undergirds this skill. Understanding the placement of objects in groups and sequences, as used in the teaching and development of number concepts, depends upon perception of form and space. The symbolic expression of the quantitative and linear relationships in mathematics is language; this involves psycholinguistic abilities, as does English. The interdependence and interrelationships of these three functions—cognitive, perceptual, and psycholinguistic—are not yet fully understood. When a child has a severe deficit in one of these functions, however, there is likely to be some degree of accompanying dysfunction elsewhere. The full extent of these relationships will be revealed even more in the future, as testing procedures improve.

When the child fails to progress in spite of good learning conditions, this is the teacher's cue to extend the search for the learning difficulty beyond the cognitive area. A perceptual-motor and/or tactile-kinesthetic dysfunction may be interfering with learning. When such dysfunction is present, it tends to be pervasive.[1] There may be psycholinguistic deficits.

"Count backwards from twenty," I said to Tom, age seven, a learning disabled (LD) child, in an effort to help him with the problem of "twenty minus three." The task was beyond him. "Count forward from zero to twenty," I urged. This he did with ease. However, when I suggested that he continue counting to one hundred, he did so, but only with frequent prompting.

Like many children who are referred because of poor school work, Tom was found to be a boy of normal intelligence.[2] His responses to the Illinois Test of Psycholinguistic Abilities subtests at the representational level demonstrated understanding of concepts and symbols appropriate for his age, supporting the

---

[1] A. Jean Ayres, "Interrelations among Perceptual-Motor Abilities in a Group of Normal Children," *The American Journal of Occupational Therapy*, No. 5 XX (November-December 1966) 288-292.

[2] Lloyd M. Dunn, *Peabody Picture Vocabulary Test*, Form A. (Minneapolis, Minn.: American Guidance Service, 1965); Richard L. Slosson, *Slosson Intelligence Test for Children and Adults* (East Aurora, N.Y.: Slosson Educational Publication, 1963).

results of his intelligence tests. His score was significantly below normal, however, on one of the subtests at the nonsymbolic level.[3] Here the child is required to repeat a series of digits after the examiner. Tom was rated below the five-year-old level. The average seven-year-old child is able to repeat aloud after the instructor a series of five digits and a sentence containing twelve words, maintaining the given sequence without additions or omissions.

OCCASIONALLY a child may have such an extreme disability in auditory memory that he is able to repeat only three or four digits and to maintain the correct word order in very short sentences. Word order is one of the four main language devices.[4] A child who uses defective syntax is greatly handicapped in his oral communication and in his thinking. Such a child frequently does not even attempt to say many words and phrases, but instead fills in with "noise" and speaks so rapidly that the listener is unable to recognize just how his speech differs from the normal pattern. The listener tends to "fill in" automatically, the missing parts for himself. "A reduced or incomplete English sentence (spoken by a child) seems to constrain the English-speaking adult to expand it into the nearest properly formed completed sentence."[5] The child, by this language behavior, inhibits the natural correctional responses of the adult listener and unwittingly maneuvers himself into a vicious circle whereby his own uncorrected speech, through the process of feedback, perpetuates his language errors.

Sometimes such a child is able to learn and work with visual symbols, but shows almost no carryover of learning when the material is presented orally — that is, when he must understand and use auditory symbols exclusively.

David, age nine, was a boy with psycholinguistic deficits in all areas, but with severe deficits in all the auditory areas. He was given the "add one" combinations to study and was told to follow them visually on the worksheet while listening to the tape on which the answers were recorded. In a few days, David was able to follow the problems on the worksheet, giving all the correct answers. When the book was closed, however, and he was asked some of these combinations orally, he was at a complete loss. It seemed he didn't understand the statement of the same problems he had read and answered easily.

David was again given the "add one" combinations to study, using the worksheet and tape recorder. This time, however, the problem, as well as the answer, was stated on the tape; *e.g.*, "Three plus one equals what? (Pause.) Four." After a few days' practice, the combinations were presented visually, and then orally. David answered correctly.

---

[3] Samuel A. Kirk and James J. McCarthy, *The Illinois Test of Psycholinguistic Abilities, Experimental Edition* (Urbana: University of Illinois, 1961).

[4] Carl A. Lefevre, *Linguistics and the Teaching of Reading* (New York: McGraw-Hill, 1964), p. 8.

[5] Roger Brown and Ursula Bellugi, "Three Processes in the Child's Acquisition of Syntax," *New Directions in the Study of Language,* edited by Eric H. Lenneberge (Cambridge, Mass.: The M.I.T. Press, 1966), p. 144.

ARITHMETIC AND LANGUAGE SKILLS

WHEN the normal child can work problems which are presented to him on a worksheet, he can do these same problems when they are presented orally, although possibly not as quickly. The normal child automatically connects the written symbol with the spoken word. When he is learning to add, and he looks at $+\frac{3}{1}$ he says to himself, "Three plus one equals — ?" or "Three and one are — ?" The LD child, on the other hand, is not always able to do this or doesn't do it because it is difficult. He merely "looks," without the accompanying inner speech.

This experience with the normal child may lead the teacher to expect this same behavior and response from all children. This "expectation" may be entirely unconscious until the teacher is confronted with a "David's" seemingly paradoxical behavior. The teacher needs to read the problem to the child, then have the child read aloud several times with him until the child is able to read the problem aloud by himself. This reading aloud by the child gives the child visual input, audio input, and tactile-kinesthetic motor input.[6]

It will be a long time before the "Davids" will be able to state the problems subvocally to themselves. Practice that includes both listening to the instructor and then repeating aloud with him is an important first step toward learning to use verbal mediators to solve problems necessary for abstract thinking — that is, thinking with symbols.[7] This subvocalizing, or verbal kinesthesis may well be an important factor in the retention and reproduction of both verbal and nonverbal series. A. R. Luria comments that in pathological states of the cortex, normal kinesthetic stimuli (of tongue and mouth) must reach the cerebral cortex during perception of an auditory or visual series for normal retention and reproduction of that series.[8] This observation, although derived from observation of adults with known organic pathology, is interesting and raises the provocative question, "How important may the presence or absence of kinesthetic stimuli of the mouth and tongue be in relation to the learning of sequences of the LD child?"

David needs to learn to read because he appears to understand the written word better than he does the spoken word. With his extreme auditory memory deficit, one would prognosticate poor reading ability, as one would from the presence of his visual memory deficit.[9] A child with David's deficits does appear to present a teaching paradox. The auditory memory deficit impedes the learning of

---

[6] William C. Jordan, "Prime-O-Tec: The New Reading Method," *Academic Therapy Quarterly*, II (Summer 1967), 248-250; Cecil Ann Rowe, "Using the Tape Recorder," *Academic Therapy Quarterly*, III (Spring 1968), 171.

[7] Alexander R. Luria, *The Role of Speech in the Regulation of Normal and Abnormal Behavior* (New York: Liveright Publishing, 1961).

[8] A. R. Luria, *Human Brain and Psychological Processes* (New York: Harper and Row, 1966), pp. 314-316.

[9] Barbara D. Bateman, *Interpretation of the 1961 Illinois Test of Psycholinguistic Abilities* (Seattle, Wash.: Special Child Publications, 1968), p. 47; Corrine E. Kass, "Some Psychological Correlates of Severe Reading Disability (Dyslexia)," *Selected Studies on the Illinois Test of Psycholinguistic Abilities* (copyright, 1963, by the authors: D. J. Sievers, J. J. McCarthy, J. L. Olson, B. D. Bateman, and C. E. Kass), 87-95.

oral language and communication skills, which in turn has a deleterious effect upon his intellectual development. His visual memory, although limited, needs to be recognized as an asset and the channel through which he can learn, including learning to read. "The visual symbol in the beginning appears to be the stimulus to elicit the auditory memory as a conditioned reflex. In time this 'starter' no longer seems to be necessary."[10]

A little reading is a great aid to learning, as seen by David's response in the following lesson: One big box and one little box were placed on the table before him. He was told, "Show me the big box," then, "Show me the little box." He performed correctly. He was then told, "Show me the box that is *not* big," and, "Show me the box that is *not* little." David was confused by the "not" in these directives. The following words were then put on cards: "big," "not little," "little," "not big." David first read the cards; he was then handed the card on which was written "not little" and was told, "Place this card beside the box that is 'not little.'"

David caught on quickly. Before the end of the hour the instructor was able to place two big red boxes, two little red boxes, two big blue boxes, and two little blue boxes in random order on the table and to say to David, now eliminating the use of the cards, "Show me the boxes that are not red and that are not little." The boy responded correctly. For the "Davids" the slogan must be, "Print it and say it."

SOMETIMES a child whose auditory memory is better than his visual memory responds in the opposite way. This may be true even though his auditory memory is only relatively "superior"; testing scores having indicated disability in both areas.

In answer to the problem, "Nancy could not read because she broke her _____?" Jim spontaneously answered, "Glasses!" However, when he turned his attention to four drawings — a girl with a broken arm, a pair of glasses, a newspaper, and a shattered cup — he placed a mark on the broken cup, erased it, commented on the broken arm, but rejected this picture as the answer, and left the question unanswered. When Jim was encouraged to give his verbal answer before looking at the pictures and to match the picture to this verbal answer, he did much better. Such a child needs to be encouraged to rely on his (verbal) thinking. He should be given printed work that has only correct answers — never a choice between correct and incorrect answers.

Bob, another LD boy, age nine, who was referred for tutoring was, like Tom, a boy of normal intelligence. His responses to the Illinois Test of Psycholinguistic Abilities, six representational level subtests, demonstrated understanding of concepts and symbols appropriate to his age. He showed, however, a significant visual-memory deficit. In this subtest the child is asked to observe for five seconds a series of geometric shapes placed horizontally on a tray in

---

[10] Florence A. Sharp, "i.t.a. and Speech and Language Problems," *The Initial Teaching Alphabet and the World of English* (Hempstead, New York: Initial Teaching Alphabet Foundation, Hofstra University, 1966), pp. 189-195. Proceedings of the Second Annual International Conference on the Initial Teaching Alphabet.

front of him. The shapes are then scrambled and the child is requested to replace them in the original sequence.

Bob was able to count forward by one's to one hundred, but he was not able to count forward by ten's, five's, two's, etc., and he had difficulty counting backwards by one's from one hundred. He easily memorized linear measurement but was unable to use this information, as is the normal child of his age.[11]

Two yardsticks were laid end to end. "How many feet long are they?" he was asked. "Place the foot rulers alongside the yardsticks to find out." Bob put down the first ruler, allowing it to extend four inches beyond the end of the first yardstick. When he put down the last foot ruler, it extended eight inches beyond the end of the second yardstick. Unaware that he was not "matching" the rulers to the yardsticks, he announced, "Seven feet."

A piece of cash-register tape was folded to mark out eight spaces and was placed horizontally in front of Bob. He was able to count the spaces. When given the directives, "Point to the end of the third space," "Point to the beginning of the fifth space," etc., his uncertain and random pointing showed that he was confused.

A substantial relationship has been found between poor mathematical ability and perceptual motor deficits, especially with the syndromes of perceptual deficit of form and space and with the deficit of integration of the two sides of the body.[12] The visual-memory subtest in which Bob demonstrated a significant deficit involves form and space perception, specifically of horizontally placed objects. The difficulty involved in the visual perception of horizontally placed geometric forms and the horizontally placed cash-register tape may have some relationship to inadequate integration of left and right visual fields. Undoubtedly more complex neural functions are involved.[13]

Since the source of Bob's visual-motor perceptual dysfunction might be this inability to adequately integrate the right and left visual fields, it occurred to me to place the "spaced off" cash-register tape vertically on the table, centered to correspond with the midline of Bob's body. This eliminated the need for side to side eye movement. One could expect, therefore, that the "visual field" would then be relayed almost exclusively to one hemisphere of the brain and therefore be received clearly. Bob's response was electric. He marked the spaces as requested without difficulty.

When the visual-memory subtest was readministered, with the modification that this time the tray holding the geometric shapes was placed vertically and centered with the midline of Bob's body, instead of being placed horizontally, he obtained a normal score.

---

[11] Jean Piaget, *How Children Form Mathematical Concepts*, reprint from *Scientific American*, November 1953 (San Francisco, Calif.: W. H. Freeman, 1953).

[12] A. Jean Ayres, "Patterns of Perceptual-Motor Dysfunction in Children: A Factor Analytic Study," *Perceptual and Motor Skills*, XX (1965), 335-368.

[13] Personal communication from A. Jean Ayres.

SENSORY-MOTOR

This subtest was again administered a week later, using the standard procedure, that is, horizontal placement of the tray holding the geometric shapes, and Bob obtained a normal score. One may assume that the viewing of the vertical placement of the geometric shapes allowed him the experience of perceiving these shapes clearly, noting their characteristics. Having once identified the shapes, he could now recognize them under "difficult" conditions, that is, in horizontal placement.

A small amount of practice working with the number line placed vertically, and working with mathematical problems presented vertically, enabled Bob to learn. Following this experience he was able to do his mathematical assignments without regard to "the positioning" of the work.

This dysfunction appears to be associated with a marked developmental lag in the maturation of the vestibular and postural reflexes. This may then be ameliorated in some children by means of an intensive neurodevelopmental activity program.[14] Such a program is vitally important to a child like Bob. While correction is the ideal treatment, the teacher may need to use a compensatory device, such as positioning materials, to make learning possible.

MATHEMATICS is a language and therefore its oral and written forms are, among other things, an expression of psycholinguistic as well as reasoning ability. An auditory or a visual memory deficit will interfere with the effective use of both mathematical and language symbols.

The vocabulary of grade-school mathematics is relatively limited. The four basic processes of calculation in arithmetic are counting. The counting sequences are orderly and logical. Mathematics is a more precise and consistent and reality-oriented language than English, and it is free from the complicated linguistic features of English. A teacher, therefore, can expect that a child with normal reasoning ability, who demonstrates a linguistic disability of the type demonstrated by Tom or Bob, may be able to learn the language of grade-school mathematics more easily than he may develop normal facility in English.

Learning the language of arithmetic, like learning any language, "is not simply a matter of learning words and symbols, it is a matter of correctly relating words and symbols to the things, events, or ideas for which they stand in our culture."[15] According to Joyce O. Hertzler, "The very act of identification involves classification."[16]

With the internalizing of language there is a resultant cognitive development. "The learning and utilization of categories represents one of the most elementary and general forms of cognition by which man adjusts to his environment.[17] In

---

[14] *Ibid.*

[15] Eileen M. Churchill, *Counting and Measuring* (Toronto: University of Toronto Press, 1961), p. 79.

[16] Joyce O. Hertzler, *A Sociology of Language* (New York: Random House, 1965), p. 40.

[17] Jerome S. Bruner, Jacqueline J. Goodnow, and George A. Austin, *A Study of Thinking* (New York: John Wiley and Sons, Science Editions, 1967), p. 2.

the mastery of specific types of problems, "learning sets" are developed which can then be brought to still more complex problems.[18] As the child learns to use mathematical language and master its many counting sequences, he will be able to handle number concepts with increasing skill. The mastery of mathematical language will also aid him in the learning of the more complex patterns and sequences of English.

In order to relate the mathematical symbols to the things and events for which they stand, all counting in the beginning and for an extended period should be done exclusively with clear structures such as Cuisenaire rods.[19] Some educators stress the importance of introducing new material through an extended period of free play.[20] The child may build with the rods in ways that are seemingly unrelated to mathematics, "but six to eight weeks spent in this free play will pay handsome dividends."[21] This free play allows the child to take the materials into his mind, mentally swallowing and digesting them.

TO LEARN, the child needs to use more than his eyes and ears. Both visual and motor experiences appear to be necessary for the development of a cognitive map of the environment essential for effective goal-directing motility.[22] Furthermore, when the child is using his eyes and ears and moving about and handling things, he is receiving vital information which his motor sensations provide. Motility, the fumblings, the trials and errors of exploration of the world about him are but the early phase of a long process which, in its advanced state, culminates in the highest mental processes — that is, learning to think and developing insight.[23]

The standard Cuisenaire rods, with the base of one centimeter, have been found to be satisfactory for teaching normal children. Larger rods, i.e., with a base of one inch or more, are, however, easier to handle, especially for the child with poor motor coordination. There is a relative difference in weight between the shortest and the longest standard Cuisenaire rods; the actual increase in weight, however, is slight. All the rods feel "light." With larger rods (base of one inch or more), the shorter and longer rods, when lifted and compared, are "felt" as light and heavy. Thus another meaningful and usable dimension is incorporated into the rods when their size is increased.

This is of special importance since "the role of proprioceptive experience

---

[18] Harry F. Harlow and Margaret Kuenne, *Learning to Think*, reprint from *Scientific American*, August 1949 (San Francisco, Calif.: W. H. Freeman, 1949).

[19] Information concerning these rods may be obtained from Cuisenaire Company of America, Inc., 235 East 50th Street, New York, New York.

[20] John Holt, *How Children Learn* (New York: Pitman, 1967).

[21] C. Gattegno, *Arithmetic: A Teacher's Introduction to Cuisenaire-Gattegno Methods* (New York: Cuisenaire Company, 1961), pp. 9-10.

[22] Henry Glietman, *Place-Learning*, reprint from *Scientific American*, October 1963 (San Francisco, Calif.: W. H. Freeman, 1963).

[23] Harlow and Kuenne, *loc. cit.*

in learning has not always received sufficient attention."[24] The messages received by the brain from the activity of the interoceptors, situated in the walls of internal body organs, and the proprioceptors, situated in the muscles and tendons, yield information about events which is at least as important as information received from the eyes and ears (the extroceptors).[25]

The only way the child can become aware of the dimensions of lightness and heaviness, roughness and smoothness, roundness and flatness, rhythm and order is through movement information relayed to the central nervous system in terms of proprioceptive sensations. Lightness and heaviness are experienced in terms of muscle effort needed to lift an object, roughness and smoothness in terms of the resistance offered to movement by various surfaces, rhythms and order in terms of a series of sensations.[26]

Since the LD child frequently has perceptual-motor deficits, he is apt to avoid many activities, such as using and manipulating materials in his free play, which normal children find pleasurable. He therefore needs to work with real things, to "fill out" his experiences.

The child's work with the rods on his desk is visible to all. This allows for more immediate guidance than does written notations. The child himself can often correct his own errors or "get started" by seeing how another child is working. He may, at times, be directed or taught by a classmate. Such a "child-teacher" is often more effective than the regular teacher, merely because he, like the learner, is a child.[27]

WHEN the child works exclusively with symbols, it is often difficult to determine, by his correct and incorrect answers alone, just where he is in his "understanding." The way a child goes about working out a problem with the Cuisenaire rods may enable the teacher to see the world through the child's eyes. This is often a moving and challenging experience.

Jeff, a ten-year-old fourth grader, after some play with the Cuisenaire rods, was told, "Find all the rods that are the same length as this black one." Jeff proceeded to pick up each rod and, one by one, methodically place it beside the black rod for comparison. When he finished and had all the black rods side by side in a row on the desk in front of him, he made no comment.

Again, Jeff was told, "Find all the rods the same length as this yellow one." He again began the laborious comparison, but about halfway through this procedure he suddenly gathered up all the remaining yellow rods, showing by this sudden and sure action that he now had insight into the fact that "rods of the same color are the same length."

Jeff had discovered that there was one consistent feature present in the rods.

---

[24] Churchill, *op. cit.*, p. 20.
[25] *Ibid.*, pp. 20-21.
[26] *Ibid.*, p. 21.
[27] Personal communication from Dr. Milton H. Erickson, Phoenix, Arizona.

He would need to repeat this experience of matching the rods in order to consolidate this learning, since practice after insight, not before, makes perfect.[28]

The next step would be for Jeff to discover the sequential relationships between the different colored rods. Then, and then only, would he have the understanding of number and sequence that is the foundation for work with numbers — *i.e.*, adding, subtracting, etc. This understanding must preferably precede or be developed along with the learning and practice of the counting sequences.

Finding out where the child "is" is beautifully illustrated by the story of Dorothy, a sixth grader. She was asked to determine the number of rods she would have to use to make two equal rows of rods, with no rods left over. She started with the problem of six rods. Dorothy counted out, from the pile, six rods, which she made into two rows of three rods each. For the next step, she pushed all the rods back into the pile, counted out seven rods, and found that seven would not work. She pushed the seven rods back into the pile. She counted out eight rods and continued in this manner until she was ready to work with fifteen rods. Finally, for the first time, she added one more rod to her pile of fourteen to make fifteen. This more efficient process she continued to twenty-four. She then made another important step forward. She said, "Twenty-five won't work — twenty-six will work," and she continued in this manner up to thirty-six. From that point on she named only the even numbers that would work.[29]

AN EMPHASIS on the counting sequences in the teaching of arithmetic is important. The four basic processes of calculation in arithmetic are counting processes:

1. Adding is counting beyond a known point in the number series.
2. Subtracting is counting backwards from a known point or counting between two known points.
3. Multiplying is counting forward in groups.
4. Dividing is counting backwards in groups.

Once the child understands this, adding, subtracting, multiplying, and dividing cease to be an enigma. The child works with confidence and interest, knowing that with a little patience and care he can use the rods, the number line, or his fingers to make any of these four basic calculations. This is a considerable accomplishment that is most satisfying, but too rarely demonstrated by the child of today.

With practice, these sequences are soon learned by the normal child, and he can see how the adding combinations and times tables give him facts to use as short cuts. The LD child, on the other hand, for whom any kind of sequencing may present difficulty, does not find it easy to keep his counting in order, even when using his fingers.

---

[28] Irvin Rock, *Repetition and Learning*, reprint from *Scientific American*, August 1958 (San Francisco, Calif.: W. H. Freeman, 1958).

[29] John Holt, *How Children Fail* (New York: Pitman, 1964), pp. 121-123.

SENSORY-MOTOR

When the normal child learns to count forward, it follows that he can reverse the process and count backwards. He may not do this as quickly or skillfully as he counted forward, but he can do it. The "automatic habit chain," once established, is two-directional. This does not hold for the child like Tom or Bob who may be able to count forward to a given number but be unable to trace his way back along the same path — that is, count backwards.

When the normal child has learned to count by one's, he finds it relatively easy to count by ten's or to skip every other number and count by two's, but this is not so for a Tom or a Bob. Such a child may learn to count forward by ten's, from zero to one hundred. He does not, however, carry over this learning so that he can count forward by ten's — from one to ninety-one, from two to ninety-two, etc. All the variations of each counting sequence must therefore be taught with the same amount of care and drill that is traditionally reserved for the presentation of an entirely new task.

The teacher will find, however, that each subsequent counting sequence is learned more quickly. This suggests that the associations have been made — that is, there are "links" and an "automatic habit chain" — but that these associations made by the LD child are much weaker than those made by the normal child. The normal child is able to carry over learning from a main task to variations of this task without direct training. The normal child's responses are so easily thought of as natural, and therefore expected, that it is often difficult to observed that the LD child's responses are different.

Because our numerical system has the base of ten, the counting series by one's or groups — ten's, five's, etc. — has a repetitive and internal consistency which results in simplicity of the patterns, rendering them easy to recognize. For these reasons, numbers are the ideal material to use to give an LD child confidence in his ability, in spite of his handicaps, to learn sequences. Once this confidence is developed, the child will carry it over to the learning of sequences and series in other areas.

Outer Space of the Inner Child

Mary Lu Kost

THE ROOM is quiet. It is crucial spelling-test time in the first grade. "The first word is *hat*," the teacher says. "Put on the hat." From his isolation corner toward the back of the room, hyperactive, effervescent little Marvin yells out, "I know! H-a-t!"

"Hush, Marvin. We don't say it out loud." But the teacher nods and winks an affirmative to the child. In six weeks of spelling lessons, he has not yet spelled a word correctly. *Maybe he's finally getting it*, the teacher thinks. As the children file out, she reaches eagerly for Marvin's small booklet. How could it be? Once again, he had not spelled one word correctly. But what about the word *hat*? He must have that right. But there it was: *t-h-a*. *The* was spelled *h-e-t; can* was *a-n-c*. All the letters were there, but they were in scrambled order. Marvin could spell orally, a sequence in time, but he could not write the letters in the same correct sequence in space on his paper.

Sixteen-year-old Greg was asked to draw a map of his home town, San Francisco, with the bay and soaring Golden Gate and San Francisco Bay bridges. He drew a wavy line down the right side of the paper to represent the land mass of the Pacific coastline, and then he stretched two bridges from that shoreline out into the ocean. The bridges hung in space like two giant drydocks. He knew the bridges were there. He had crossed them many times. He was unable, however, to relate them to the land masses.

Then there are the numerous children, every teacher knows, who appear to be reading well in the first two preprimers where the word configurations are markedly dissimilar. They have relied solely on those little configuration boxes to discriminate words. But now new words appear in the third preprimer, the primer, and the first reader. They are not so different, Thus, *airplane* and *surprise*, *shop* and *stop*, *store* and *chair*, *play* and *help*, *what* and *want* appear the same to these children. Since they are often intelligent, they know what word to "read" because of the context. Visually handicapped Mike could "read" all three preprimers with few errors, but he couldn't recognize one word from those books when they were presented on flashcards with no context clues.

In math, the subtraction problems are added, and the missing addend is the sum. A "10" might be written "01," and the teens all come out reversed: 21, 31, 41, 51, 61, etc.; or the answer to the problem, "23 + 3," might be given as "62."

In working puzzles, the child is unable to see the relationships of the shapes and sizes, and he attempts to put a rounded piece into a sharp-cornered opening. He may recognize only a part of something and be unable to synthesize the parts into a whole object. He may recognize a square, for example, but be unable to generalize the concept of squareness by drawing it, walking it out, or forming it with pegs. He can see that it has four sides, but he can't place these four sizes into the proper relationships with one another to form the square. He does not perceive the relationship between the square and the shape of a window or a card table or a cube.

The teacher is frequently angry with the child for his "obstinancy" or his "stupidity" in failing to follow directions. He won't put his name on the *top* of the paper, he fails to fold the paper *lengthwise*, or he can't do free cutting as the other children can. His "hearts" are simply crude half-circles or they are pointed at both ends. He is unable to put several numbered pages together in the correct order to form a book; even though he can count efficiently, the pages are upside-down, backwards, and not in the correct sequence. He may have satisfactory coordination for "coloring in" something but be unable to make a representational drawing. The house resembles a tent. The windows are all on top of the door.

In whatever way the problem may manifest itself in the child's schoolwork, the basis for the confusion is the lack of an integrated, generalized, stable concept of space. He confuses the positions in space of the objects. Thus, *top, bottom, up, down, right, left, under, over*, etc., may be unclear or the relationships between the objects may be confused. The child can't put the scissors *beside* the book, the paper on *top* of his desk, the plus mark *between* the two 2's; or he just can't see the difference between the *long* block and the *short* block.

The objects in the problem child's spatial world will not remain static. Thus, sometimes his letters, words, numerals, or math problems are correct, and at other times they are reversed or twisted or scrambled. One boy said, "The words just don't stand still. They make me dizzy." If the initial perception of the word is inaccurate, if the letters appear jumbled to the child, there cannot possibly be an accurate recall of the word (or the equation).

LET'S GO BACK and try to understand how the normal child learns to perceive his space world of position, sizes, distances, relationships, etc., so that he has instant understanding of these elements of his environment. Everything in our environment derives its position on this earth from ourselves and our relation to the forces of gravity. In the celestial world there is no up, no down. There is no right, or left, no infront of, no behind. The pull of gravity gives us the concept of down. It is the one constant in our space world. As we crawl and learn to balance ourselves in the upright position in relation to this pull, we begin to form concepts of other directions. That which is near our feet — drawn by gravity — is down. That which is toward our heads and away from the pull of gravity is up. Objects have right sides only because they are on the right side of us. Words start on the left of the paper, not because the paper has any individual leftness, but because of the paper's relationship to the left side of our bodies and because our culture dictates a left-right sequence. *Behind you* is by your back where you can't see it. *Behind the chair* is at the side of the chair away from your body where you cannot see wholly. It could even be near the front of the chair, but because you cannot see it entirely and it is away from your body, you say that it is behind the chair. Thus, objects in our environment have directions only in relation to us.

The first prerequisite for a stable space world, therefore, is the balance of the organism in relation to the earth. When the child first lifts his head up from his bed (from the prone position on his stomach), it wobbles and flops down again. With repeated practice and clear kinesthetic messages from his muscles, tendons, and the semicircular canals of his ears, etc., he finally learns a balanced position of his head in space and derives his first concepts of the up and down space. *Up* is directly above his line of vision when his head is balanced. *Down* is the surface of his bed. As the child learns to crawl, he has to make some adjustments to keep his head and body balanced as he moves across the floor. Again, as he pulls himself upright and begins to toddle, he must reorganize his body balance to keep from falling. As the child develops through motor learnings, he is continually learning to adjust his body to balance in space.

As he achieves stable balance in vertical space, and thus his up-down world, he begins to develop his horizontal or side and front-back space also. Without the balance he has no distinct horizontal space. In crawling he is moving horizontally. In order to crawl with any speed or agility, he has to learn more than the infantile simultaneous movement of his limbs; he has to learn how to operate the two sides of his body separately and how to coordinate the two extremes of his body — the arms and the legs — at the same time. Without the balance, he could not realize any difference between the two sides of his body. He finds how one side can counterbalance the other. He can reach out with one hand while the other is still on the floor. When he leans forward, if he shifts his supporting hand, he will not fall. He can hold a toy with one hand while he explores it with the other. He learns a thousand ways of using his hands and legs together or reciprocally to gain efficiency of movement. He reaches for a toy on the right with his right hand because he has learned that this is faster, more efficient. In this way he achieves a firm laterality and an understanding of the many ways in which he can coordinate the sides of his body.

The child knows the difference between his right side and his left side now. He may have even found one side to be more efficient than the other, and thus he may have attained a dominance of one side over the other. This dominance probably helps him to stabilize his feelings for the relationships of his right and left sides.

At the same time that the child is establishing bilateral coordinations and laterality, he is also learning about all of his body parts: where they are, how to move them, what sensations they receive, how much room they require in space. Body image is a necessary part of learning laterality, bilateral control, etc.

THE CHILD first uses all of his senses to explore an object or a space. The motor learnings predominate at first. He learns the size of the room by the amount of energy and time it takes to crawl across it. He learns the shape of objects by manipulating them. He learns what his body can do by moving through space in many ways. As he integrates the elements of these performances and uses them in a variety of situations, he also achieves a fine visual skill. As he integrates the elements of these performances and uses them in a variety of situations, he also achieves a fine visual skill. As he achieves perceptual maturity, with his eyes alone he can judge distance and size relationships, positions, textures, and weight. He begins to explore with his eyes the way he previously did with his hands, and he integrates the new visual information with all his motor and sensory background. Ocular acuity, motility, and perception must now be extremely accurate to afford a match with the information the child has hitherto accumulated via motor, tactual, olfactory, gustatory, and auditory channels. The visual mode then becomes the most rapid, efficient mode of learning and the one taken for granted by our schools today. If there is not an adequate perceptual-motor match of incoming stimuli and information with subsequent motor movement, the directions of the child's spatial word are confused. He is unsure of the top-right and the bottom-left side of the paper, and the letters have no stable relationships, one with the other.

Now he has achieved balance, laterality, bilateral coordination, body image, accurate visual perception, and he can make a perceptual-motor match. With these perceptions stabilized, he can accurately relate objects in space to himself. The sentence starts on his *left*; he is to stand on the *right* side of his desk; he is to put his hands *behind* his back; he is to hold his book *on* his lap. We call this "position in space" or "directionality."

Finally, he is able to project these relationships out into space and see how these objects relate to each other. The teacher wants him to start at the top of his paper — which is related to the top of his head if he holds the paper vertically. The spoon is to the *right* of the dish because it is to his right also. The *c* is on the *left*, the *t* is on the *right*, and the *a* is *between* the *c* and the *t*. Now the letters and numerals remain constant — in the same static positions — and the child is enabled to gain instant recognition from a stable, visual memory of the word or equation. His response to these objects is automatic, requiring no analysis.

He learns to compare sizes and shapes of objects by putting them one on top of or inside the other. The spoon is so little that it takes many, many spoonfuls of sand to fill the big cup. He can pick up the short block easily, but it takes both arms and a change of body posture to carry the long block. He would rather have three pieces of candy because that is more. That car looks smaller, but it is just farther away. In learning to relate objects precisely, he has gained the basis for quantitative relationships — and a foundation for school math.

To gain these understandings, the child has to do thousands of manipulations and comparisons. But what if he came from a deprived home where he never had the toys, the kitchen pans, the cups, the variety of furniture, etc., with which to make these comparisons? In such a situation, suppose he was never given the encouragement to explore nor the language to parallel his explorations? What if he is so distracted by figure-ground confusion that he is unable to concentrate on the explorations or on the sensations he is receiving. What if his tactile receptors are not supplying him with accurate information? What if his erratic ocular movements cause his visual perceptions of form, distance, and space to be inaccurate or distorted? What if he receives all of these sensory messages correctly but is unable to integrate them, to relate the many messages in order to make a perceptual-motor match, thereby directing his further explorations? What if he is still in Piaget's "empirical" or trial-and-error stage of space awareness wherein he is still trying out these yet unlearned relationships? There could be many "ifs." He could have gone through the motions of feeling, looking, hearing, moving, etc., but never really learning in a cognitive manner essential to accurate perception and thus to the establishment of a stable space world.

THIS IS, of necessity, but a capsule explanation of the development of spatial concepts, but these premises are singularly essential to an understanding of how to approach the training of children with deficiencies in spatial orientation. The first step in alleviating the child's spatial problems must be a diagnosis of where the problem lies. Because of the previously mentioned stages of spatial development, the child's problem in spatial relations might really be in his lack of understanding concerning the position of objects in space. The problem might go back to a need for a stable laterality. If both of these areas are disturbed so that the child lacks a feeling for horizontal space, then you must go back to balance and to vertical space to begin training. If the child lacks knowledge of his body in space, then training in body image must be initiated. If he is severely disturbed, has global problems, or is six years old or under, it would be best to concentrate on the training in these basic essential areas before training is begun in position in space and spatial relations. If the child is older or is less confused, training in spatial concepts may parallel that in body image, laterality, and balance.

For diagnostic purposes, one could use the Marianne Frostig Developmental Test of Visual Perception, the Purdue Perceptual Rating Scale, the Sprains Multiple-Choice, Bender Gestalt, Valett's Psychoeducational Survey of Basic Learning Abilities, or Beery's Developmental Test of Visual-Motor Integration.[1]

When you are concerned with testing a total class of children and the above tests are not available to you, a series of simple tests and observations will give you clues to the child's problems. A foundation can be formed by using the Winter Haven Lions' Perceptual Forms Test, the Bender Visual-Motor Gestalt Test, and Goodenough's Draw-a-Man. The Horst Reversal Test is also helpful.[2] To these aids you may add representative dittos of spatial relations, position in space, visual-motor, figure-ground, sequence of shapes, etc. Several companies offer ditto masters that focus on these problems, or you can make up your own. When there is still a further question of the child's ability in one of these areas, use more exercises from different levels of that ability.

Observations of the child's performance will give you more clues. Watch his static and dynamic balance, his flexibility, coordination of body parts, cutting and assemblying abilities, mirroring movements, etc. Watch how he follows directions when instructed to go over, under, or behind something. Can he relate two objects, putting one in front of, on top of, or alongside another? Can he place his own body in relation to his desk as you direct him? Can he follow your directions?

---

[1] See references for sources of tests.

[2] The Horst Reversal Test may be found in *Predicting Reading Failure*, by Katrina De-Hirsch, Jeannette J. Jansky, and William S. Langford (New York, N.Y.: Harper and Row, 1966).

SENSORY-MOTOR

When a profile is formed of the results of these tests and observations, you will have a basis for knowing where the child's problem lies and where to begin training.

When norms of behavior for the various skills and tests are not available, simply rate the test performance of your class on a curve, and then consider the lower scores as indicative of a deficiency. You might collect the test papers of the problem child and your notes about him, and then sit down with the school psychologist for help on the evaluation of your data.

Because the ability to concentrate and discriminate figure from the background in all sensory modes is so basic to all sensory discrimination and thus to learning, figure-ground must be one of the first considerations. The highly distractible hyperactive child with figure-ground problems might be referred for medical consideration of possible drug therapy. Stimulants are being used with these children to raise the synaptic resistance in the reticular formation of the brain where the sorting of incoming stimuli takes place. Children with figure-ground problems also benefit from sensory stimulation.[3] Also, their inability to sort stimuli makes a less distracting environment essential. Cut down on the visual and auditory stimuli when you want them to concentrate on learning from the three- and two-dimensional exercises. As you proceed with sensory stimulation and with perceptual training, try increasing the amount of distraction slightly with the simpler activities. Increase the amount of background stimuli with music, rhythm, or a new environment.

SINCE other chapters in this compilation deal with body image, laterality, and directionality, I will deal here only with the final stage of spatial awareness — that of the relationships of objects in space or "spatial relations." Because I am a regular-classroom teacher, most of my methods have been developed for simultaneous use with thirty first-graders and with children up to thirteen years of age who are being individually tutored. I feel strongly that we will never be able to include all of the children with perceptual-motor problems in special classrooms, and that it is therefore imperative for us to find ways to incorporate these training methods into the regular classroom.

Understanding of size and shape comparisons of objects really begins in the basic forms. With children who have visual-perceptual problems and with normal five- and six-year-olds I start with the form templates to stabilize the concept of form and position.[4] The paper and the template must be straight on the desk. (Manila drawing paper is easier to control.) The children's posture must be balanced with both arms on the desk. It is important that they verbalize the directions as they trace the template. With the square, it might be, "Down, over, up, across." The rectangle might be, "Long, short, long, short." With the triangle, they might start at the top and go "toward the left elbow, straight across, up to the top." After they have the visual form made by the template, they follow the shape with

---

[3] A. Jean Ayres, *Perceptual-Motor Dysfunction in Children* (Cincinnati, Ohio: Greater Cincinnati Occupational Therapy Association, 1964).

[4] Winter Haven Lions project (see references); Also G. N. Getman and Elmer Kane, *The Physiology of Readiness* (Minneapolis, Minn.: P.A.S.S., 1964).

their crayon, reminding themselves to "stop, stop, stop, stop" at each corner.[5] They also trace the forms in reverse direction, varying positions, etc., for a secure perceptual-motor match. They turn the shape into a picture, reproduce the shape in a variety of sizes, and with the rectangle, they vary the dimensions. Thus, it may be made in a vertical or horizontal position, be fat or thin, large or small. The child finds the shape in his environment: the door, the table, the paper, the light fixtures, etc. He identifies or describes new objects according to the basic forms. A peanut shell is like two ovals together. A sugar cube has squares on every side.

The children love "feeling and tasting" parties. They close their eyes and put out their hands. You give each child a cracker, pebble, nut, leaf, candy, etc. They feel its texture and shape, smell its aroma, rub or shake it by their ears, taste it, and finally look at it so that the item is described in every way possible.

In teaching the handling of objects, emphasize positions and relationships. For example, when you are teaching cutting you might say: "Hold the paper with your thumb on top. Hold the scissors straight up and down and cut with the inside of the scissors." When you instruct the children in carrying a chair say: "Hold the back of the chair with the legs down so that you won't hit anyone." Demonstrate each action before you verbalize it. Then have the children repeat it when you ask: "How do we hold the paper?"

Use errands as opportunities to teach spatial relations. Give each direction carefully, being sure the child understands each step. The child with severe problems will have enough to do to "Get the paper from on top of my desk." (One direction.) Increase the difficulty until the child can understand and perform a series of directions: "Go to the long top drawer in the back of the room and get a large piece of paper from the right-hand side." This is a complicated statement involving five directions. It should be given only to a child who has had considerable training with these terms.

Provide a firm basis for position in space and spatial relations by beginning with the position of the child's own body in relation to objects. "Stand in front of your desk. Jump over your seat." This could be presented in the form of a game similar to "Simon Says," except that the child is never made to sit out the game because he erred. He needs the practice more than do the children who are able to follow the instructions correctly. Give the directions in the spirit of: "Who can do it? Tommy can. Can you?" Use a variety of classroom objects. "Can you stand under the flag?" "Mike, can you stand in front of this pointer?" Use smaller body parts: "Put your finger under the box." "Put your hand on top of your book."

Teach the concept of *behind*. "Tommy, stand behind the flannelboard." "Where are Tommy's feet? Why can't you see them?" Tommy stands in front of the flannelboard. "Can you see all of Tommy now? Can you see all of the flannelboard? Why not?" Have the child go around the corner of the room (or out of the door) and peek back, making only his head visible to the class. "Where is Tommy's body now?" Take the children outside and note buildings that are behind

---

[5]See Newell C. Kephart on stopping in *The Slow Learner in the Classroom* (Columbus, Ohio; Charles E. Merrill, 1960).

SENSORY-MOTOR

other buildings and thus only partially visible. Have the children draw pictures of objects that are partly behind other objects.

Teach physical-education activities which utilize attention to directions. For a race: "Your feet must be behind the line." Relays: "Pass the ball under your legs then over the next child." Calisthenics: "Be sure your feet are on top of your line. Jump, turning your whole body around, and land with both feet on the line." Make up an obstacle course inside or out of doors. "Go under the board, over the rope, around the pole, and then down the slide."

Teach the relation of one child's body to that of another child. "Jerry, can you stand in front of Tommy?" "Lillian, you stand in back of Tommy," "Judy, can you stand beside Tommy?"

THE CHILD is now ready for directions concerning the relationships between objects. Give two objects to each child so the children can respond simultaneously. Remember that when only one child is moving, he is probably also the only child learning. Give directions such as, "Put the large block behind the small block," etc.

Have on hand three three-inch triangles of different colored felt. Cut enough like-colored triangles of construction paper so that each child has a similar set of three triangles. Place your triangles on the feltboard in a straight row, apexes up. The children duplicate your arrangement with their triangles, using correct position and sequence of colors. Turn your triangles into a different position while the children hide their eyes. Begin with horizontal placement, then vertical, then diagonal. This exercise may be used with a variety of different shapes: ovals, squares, rectangles, etc. Later make it more difficult by combining two or three sets of these shapes and by making more intricate designs.

Another helpful exercise is to glue matchsticks to cardboard in a variety of different relative positions and in arrangements that range from elementary to complicated formations. Begin with the simplest arrangement, placing the cardboard pattern in the chalkrack. The children use matchsticks (with the heads removed) at their desks to duplicate designs.

Paste three-inch squares of colored construction paper on a large cardboard, eighteen inches square, after the manner of Color Cubes. Each child has a cardboard that is about nine inches square and marked off in squares. He arranges one-and-one-half-inch squares of construction paper on his board to replicate your design.

Fold a square paper several times to make boxes. Color one of the corner boxes and show the children how to "mirror" this same box to all four corners. Color the other corner boxes likewise to form a symmetrical design.

Make individual six-hole pegboards of masonite sheets. They need not be framed, but one-inch boards should be nailed on the two undersides to hold the pegboard off the desk. For the pegs, cut about one-half inch off the points of single-color golf tees. To demonstrate examples for the entire class to see, for a pegboard you can use a large cardboard, a flannelboard, or you can simply draw on the blackboard, using brightly colored chalk to designate the pegs in the holes. Begin with a simple line arrangement or with a four-cornered pattern and have the children duplicate the design. Increase the difficulty of the patterns to diagonals, basic shapes, and random placements. The one rule with all of these exercises is that the child must achieve success with every task.

Another exercise that can be done with pegs is to place two pegs in holes in the pegboard and ask the child to fill the holes between the pegs. Begin with lateral and horizontal lines and then use three or more pegs to set the limits for right angles, squares, triangles, and letters such as *H* and *T*. Start with figures that have joined lines, such as *T*; introduce intersecting lines, such as +; and then go to the diagonal lines, such as *X*.

There are many manipulative puzzles and games which teach spatial relations. The geoboard uses rubber bands stretched between plastic pegs to form shapes and designs.[6] Also, there are Color Cubes, Parquetry Blocks, the Jumbo Shape Sorting Board, Graduated Shapes, Fit-a-Space, Kittie-in-the-Keg, Hammer-Nail Sets, Magnetic Basic-Form Boards, and Simplex Puzzles. Simplex Puzzles have graduated sizes of an object in mixed order on a board. Other devices are Cylinder Blocks, Math Balance, Blockbuster Blocks, Pattern Cubes, and Tic-Tac-Toe. The latter is a three-dimensional version of the old game for middle-grade children. Watch for puzzles and games which require judgments as to form, size, and placement.

SOME CHILDREN are apt to complete the puzzles of size relations without really learning anything. They merely use methods of trial and error or "hit and maybe." Teach the child who does this to feel each piece carefully with both hands. Take him through the steps of tactile and visual judgment before he attempts to find the correct solution. If he errs on the placement of a piece, ask him what is wrong with it. Present leading questions to force him to use judgment to find the correct piece. Remember that these learnings must be cognitive for permanent learning to take place.

If a child has trouble judging size relationships, use a graduated cone or a device such as Peter Porpoise. These materials are more easily felt and the size differences can be discriminated more easily because they fit so precisely one on top of the other. Remember, too, that it is often the tactile sense which is underdeveloped in the child with learning problems. He doesn't know how to use his hands to help his eyes make judgments. His tactile sense may need frequent stimulation before he will be able to use it accurately to aid his visual discrimination.

Teach comparative sizes — short, long, fat, thin — with whatever objects are available. Have the child find the biggest chair, the longest ruler, etc. Cuisenaire rods are excellent for this. Ask the child to find the longest block, the shortest block, the smallest block, the one that is larger than the black block. The children can also make symmetrical designs with the rods. Provide boxes of mixed items for them to sort according to size and form. Buttons, screws, letters, and numerals can be sorted into egg cartons. Lids can be fitted to small boxes. Frostig worksheets are excellent. There are also ditto masters designed for exercises in

---

[6] The sources of devices and materials mentioned are given at the end of this article.

spatial relations (Continental Press). Use these ditto exercises carefully, however, because they tend to become much too difficult quickly. I prefer those that form designs with dots joined by lines rather than the free-drawn ones. The connected dots control the activity, allow less chance for error, and require more precise decisions on placement. Let the child erase and change his work as often as he desires, or have extra copies handy so that he can avoid frustration when he sees his errors and wants to change them. Do not mark any of the attempts wrong, but help the child to complete each paper correctly.

Teach the apparent changes in size of objects according to their distances from vision. Have the children hold balls that are the same size at various distances, at least ten feet apart. Note the size appearance of the balls. Have the child who is farthest away advance slowly while the class observes the change in the ball size. Have a child who is closer retreat gradually so the class can see the ball diminish in size. Place different sizes of balls at various distances to compare appearances. Do the same with other objects. Sit outside and look off in the distance to compare sizes of buildings, cars, telephone poles, etc. "Is that telephone pole down the block smaller than this one near us? Use your finger to measure it. Is it as big as your finger?" Find a taller object behind a smaller one. "See that white building there? Is it the same size as that gray one? How do you know it is bigger?"

MAP MAKING can help the child to orient himself in space. Since children with spatial problems are apt to have difficulty finding their way around the school plant (as well as with map reading), try walking a specific route, dramatizing each turn, counting the number of steps. For example: "When we go out of our door to the office, we turn left." Go through these motions with the child and exaggerate the left turn, even repeating it several times. "Now let's count the steps to the corner of the building." After walking through the whole process, return to the room and use a large strip of butcher paper on the floor to recreate the trip. While you help the child draw the route, he can walk it with his fingers or using a man doll. The next step might be to draw a butcher-paper map on a table. The buildings could be cut and folded to be three-dimensional and then applied to the lines on the map. Finally, raise the map to a vertical position by hanging it from the top of the blackboard. Repeat as many stages of the process as necessary to make other maps of the room, the child's neighborhood, a store with which he is familiar, or the dairy the class visited yesterday. Maps of the child's home and yard could be made in sand or sawdust. Teach him the directions of the globe by noting the feel of the wind on a north-wind day, by deciding in which direction the flag is blowing and which windows of the room can be opened without blowing all the papers around. Older children can tie this all in to the map making.

Relief maps such as are made for the blind will help to teach the children to understand maps of terrain. Older children can make relief maps of asbestos, clay, or paper mache.

Because math is spatial and concerned with quantitative relationships, the children with spatial-relations problems will need a great deal of help in this area. Horizontal equations may be more difficult because of left-right sequencing problems. The use of vertical placement of problems may give these children more success. Missing addends and signs may be too frustrating for them. If so, you must go back to what the child does know and try to work from there. Extensive use of manipulative materials for all age levels is most important if the child is to understand quantitative relationships. He must be able to see and "feel" the differences between quantities before he will understand the abstract symbols of math. Double check to be sure the child has instant recognition of the numerals and of standard sets of dots (as on dominos), that he matches one to one in counting, and that he understands quantities — that he can give you six pencils, four crayons, etc. — before you expect him to use the abstract symbols of math equations.

For elementary-school children who are confused by math, I like the Cuisenaire rod program and John Trivett's *Mathematical Awareness*, although I prefer slightly larger rods.[7] With the rods, you first teach their size relationships and then various ways of manipulating and combining them. (Using the rods on rug samples cuts down the noise in the classroom.) Through the rods, the child comes to understand quantitative relationships before you begin to call the rods by number name; then as you teach him to make patterns or combinations, you can have him learn to write the equations which they have formed. If writing numerals is still difficult for him, plastic numerals make equations more exciting.

With the rods and plastic numerals, all of the children are working, manipulating, and with encouragement, thinking. A candy or cookie reward for each child keeps him actively participating at all times.

Don't make the mistake of thinking that these rods are only for small children. Computations with them can become very sophisticated, carrying the child through nonequivalent sets, missing addends and signs, multiplication and division, and with them the child can learn the principals of commutativity, associativity, distribution, etc.

"Lock in" each equation by manipulating the quantities and numerals in many different ways. For example, discover $2 + 2$ with rods; form it with numerals horizontally, vertically, and in right-to-left direction. Jump it. Have each child find $2 + 2$ objects in the room and arrange them on his desk. He writes it and gives it to a neighbor to find the sum. He shows it on his fingers. You show it on flashcards — again in different arrangements. Only when it is learned so thoroughly that it is automatic is the child ready to find the sums of pages of symbolic equations.

TECHNIQUES that use jumping are especially reinforcing to the perceptually handicapped child because he receives both tactile and kinesthetic stimuli. The whole class can jump in place — $2 + 2$, $5 + 1$, etc. — using a short pause between the addends to separate them. Also try jumping out addition equations on a butcher-paper number line on the floor. It can be done with the children divided into teams and using two number lines, each child receiving a prize when he ends on the correctly numbered space. Of course, no one loses; you help the less able child until he too wins the prize.

---

[7] John V. Trivett, *Mathematical Awareness* (Mount Vernon, N.Y.: Cuisenaire Company, 1962).

To help the child understand the concept of "tens," cut one-half-inch dowling into six- to eight-inch lengths. Have one wooden frame with nine single holes for nine sticks and another frame which will hold nine bundles of ten sticks. Use these sticks and frames to parallel count the correct quantity and to illustrate the position of the numerals in writing. For example, "23" would be two bundles of 10's in the ten-frame, and three 1's in the one-frame. The tens-frame is, of course, placed to the left of the ones-frame so the child learns to write the numerals in the correct order. Again, each child can show the correct number with his plastic numerals. Repeated practice on this device gives the child a visual picture of various quantities.

There are many other manipulative materials: Learning Numbers, a self-correcting item; Math Balance; Structural Arithmetic, which is a complete math program. Dr. Sigfried Englemann, of the University of Illinois, is developing a math program with culturally deprived children which shows great promise.

Reading is a task which requires a multiplicity of skills, a deficiency in any one of which could cause frustration for the child who is learning to read. Ocular motility alone is a prime factor. There are the auditory skills: discrimination, memory, and sequence in time. Figure-ground confusion can prevent the child's initial clear discrimination of the word and his attention to the task of reading. Laterality and directionality are needed to stabilize the child's spatial world and to help him understand where the word starts and how it progresses.

The child with spatial-relations problems may have difficulty discriminating words which are similar. The relationships between the letters are confusing. Is the word *play* or *help*? Is the *l* second or fourth? Is that an *a* or an *e*? This type of confusion could be the result of inaccurate discrimination of the letters in the first place. Therefore, the first step is to teach each letter so thoroughly that the child can identify it in a variety of sizes, appearances, executions, and positions. He must then understand sequence in space. This can be taught by having the child copy or repeat a pattern of blocks or felt pieces on his desk or of beads on a string. The learning is then carried on to the sequence of letters. You form the word with large letters (or simply write it on the chalkboard) and each child uses his individual manipulative letters at his desk to form the word. As a variation, one child can form his word with his letters and then scramble them into a confused order for his buddy to unscramble. Have the child form similar, easily confused words — such as *that, this*, and *the* — in a vertical column on his desk. As with the math combinations, teach the word through a variety of other devices too: tracing it, spelling it, writing it, etc. Alter its position in space. Can the child find it on a paper when it is vertical, upside-down, slanted, in capitals, typed, or written? The child must have instant visual memory of the word. Try flashing it on a screen. He must then find that word among others on his paper and draw a box around it.

Some children can be taught via a kinesthetic method. Form the word with beaded letters which the child traces with his finger. Scramble the letters and see if he can replace them correctly and then trace them again to verify his task. You might also try tracing the difficult word on the child's inner left arm, beginning by the bend of his elbow. This is a sensitive tactile area and may make him "feel" the difference in the word. More stimuli may be initiated to aid him through holding his hand while he also traces it in the same way. If he is left-handed, do it on his right arm, starting at the wrist. The different sensation derived from the wrist and the inner elbow may also reinforce left-to-right progression.

TO SUMMARIZE, children's disabilities in spatial relations, which are often evident as they are exposed to the three R's, are remediable and preventable by treating the underlying cause of the disability rather than its academic manifestation. Progression is from the concrete, manipulative third dimension to the manipulation of the abstract symbols to the two-dimensional abstract math and reading. The keys to successful remediation are the child's step-by-step successful progression, the multisensory approach, and multirepetition.

REFERENCES

Barsch, Ray H. *Achieving Perceptual-Motor Efficiency*. Seattle, Wash.: Special Child Publications, 1967.

Beery, Keith E., and Norman Buktenica. *The Developmental Test of Visual-Motor Integration*. Chicago, Ill.: Follett, 1968.

Bender, Lauretta. *Visual-Motor Gestalt Test*. New York: American Orthopsychiatric Association, 1946.

Frostig, Marianne. *Developmental Test of Visual Perception*. Palo Alto, Calif.: Consulting Psychologists Press, n.d.

──────────, and David Horne. *The Frostig Program for the Development of Visual Perception; Teachers' Guide*. Chicago, Ill.: Follett, 1964.

Goodenough, Florence. *Measurement of Intelligence*. Yonkers, N.Y.: World Book Company, 1926.

Kephart, Newell C., and Eugene B. Roach. *Purdue Perceptual Rating Scale*. Columbus, Ohio: Charles E. Merrill, 1966.

Learning Aids for Young Children in Accordance with Montessori. Chicago, Ill.: A. Daigger and Company, n.d.

Spraings, Violet. *Spraings Multiple-Choice Bender Gestalt*. Olympia, Wash.: Sherwood Press, n.d.

Vallett, Robert E. *A Psychoeducational Survey of Basic Learning Abilities*. Palo Alto, Calif.: Consulting Psychologists Press, n.d.

Winter Haven Lions Publication Committee. *Perceptual Forms; Teachers' Test Manual*. Winter Haven, Fla.: Starr Press, 1963.

MATERIALS SOURCES

Geoboard; Cuisinaire Rods: Cuisinaire Company, Mount Vernon, New York.

Color Cubes, Parquetry Blocks, Jumbo Shape Sorting Board, Graduated Shapes, Fit-a-Space, Kittie-in-the-Keg, Hammer-Nail Sets, Magnetic Basic-Form Boards, and *Simplex Puzzles:* Lakeshore Curriculum Materials Center, Oakland, California.

Cylinder Blocks; Math Balance: Daigger and Company, Chicago, Illinois.

Blockbuster Blocks: I.D.A., Citrus Heights, California.

Pattern Cubes; Tic-Tac-Toe: Creative Playthings, Inc., Princeton, New Jersey.

Learning Numbers; Peter Porpoise: Child Guidance, Bronx, New York.

Ditto Masters of Spatial Relations Exercises: Continental Press, Pasadena, California.

Structural Arithmetic: Houghton-Mifflin Company, Palo Alto, California.

ABOUT THE AUTHORS...

SHEILA DORAN BENYON is a teacher at the Briarwood School, Houston, Texas, and director of training at the Houston Child Achievement Center. She has had experience as a special-education therapist, and she has taught at both the elementary-school and the high-school levels. She is the author of *Intensive Programming for Slow Learners* (Columbus, Ohio: Chas. E. Merrill, 1968).

BEVERLY B. CASEBEER teaches the developmental first grade in the educationally handicapped program of the Inland Valley Elementary School, Orinda, California. She has extensive experience teaching both in preschool and regular primary-grade classes, and she served as director of the Head Start Test School. She is the recipient of a grant awarded by NDEA (National Defense Education Act) for teachers of disadvantaged children.

FLORIA COON-TETERS is a learning analyst with the Richmond, California, School District. Her background includes clinical and remedial work with children, both in the United States and abroad, and she has served as a consultant to professional organizations. She was general assistant of the Child Study Center, University of California, Berkeley, and has written extensively in the field of learning disabilities.

JANE FAELCHLE is a resource teacher of neurologically handicapped children in the Columbus, Ohio, public schools. She has been an elementary-school teacher of the deaf and the hard-of-hearing, as well as of children in regular classes.

LENA GITTER, a student of Maria Montessori, has traveled widely throughout the United States and Europe, conducting workshops on the Montessori Method. She has been a consultant to the United States Office of Economic Opportunity and is at present acting as consultant in education to Mayor Charles Evers of Fayette, Mississippi. She is also working to develop a Human Resource Center for the Adams-Jefferson Improvement Corporation in Natchez, Mississippi.

DONALD WILLIAM HARDY, Ed.D., is associate professor of education at the University of Redlands, Redlands, California. He has been an elementary-school teacher and was principal of Inland Valley Elementary School, Orinda, California, for seven years. He is past-president of the Orinda Education Association and was a recipient of a USOE Small Contract Grant for a research project in anthropology.

R. G. HECKELMAN, Ph.D., is coordinator of Pupil Personnel Services for Lucia Mar Unified School District, Pismo Beach, California. His published works have appeared in major educational and psychological journals. He has written and spoken extensively on special approaches, particularly the neurological-impress method, that are useful with both disabled and well-functioning readers and learners.

HAROLD B. HELMS has taught at the elementary and junior-high-school levels and is now an academic therapist with the DeWitt Reading Clinic, San Rafael, California. He is at present doing graduate work in learning problems at the University of California, Berkeley.

MARY LU KOST teaches first grade at Dry Creek School, Rio Linda, California. She has had extensive experience in teaching young children, including seven years as a kindergarten teacher and four years teaching transitional pre-first grade. She is the author of a book, *Preventing First-Grade Failure*, to be published by Charles C. Thomas.

SHIRLEY H. LINN is coordinator of perceptual training for kindergarten with the Auburn-Wasburn U.S.D. No. 437 schools in Topeka, Kansas. She has been a regular classroom teacher and a teacher for homebound children, as well as having conducted the first pilot class for neurologically impaired children in Kansas. She has published a number of articles dealing with learning impairments in young children.

EMILY BRADLEY LYONS, a reading consultant and optometric visual training technologist, is associate director of optometric assistants of the Optometric Extension Program Foundation, Duncan, Oklahoma. With her husband, the late Dr. C. Venard Lyons, she has coauthored a number of works on optometric visual training.

C. VENARD LYONS, O.D., who passed away in November 1968, was an optometrist at the Tomales Bay Visual Center, Marshall, California. He wrote and lectured extensively on optometric visual training and was for twenty years the study-group chairman in San Francisco County for the Optometric Extension Program, of which he was a charter member.

GRACE M. PETITCLERC is an educational therapist who has had many years of experience as a teacher of learning-disabled children. She has also written extensively on the subject of learning problems and is on the executive board of the Institute for Research in Childhood Health and Education, Oakland, California.

MARTHA SERIO is a consultant for the Program for Neurologically Handicapped Children in the Columbus, Ohio, public schools. She has had extensive experience as a teacher of slow learners and the neurologically handicapped and has contributed many articles to the literature in learning disabilities.

FLORENCE A. SHARP, Ph.D., is a psychologist and speech pathologist in Los Angeles, California. Her background includes extensive work in counselling and social work. She is a member of several professional organizations. Dr. Sharp, assistant clinical professor of psychiatry at Loma Linda, California, University of Medicine, has written and spoken on special learning problems, and maintains a practice in this area.

JACK WAHL, formerly an academic therapist at the DeWitt Reading Clinic, San Rafael, California is on the faculty of the College of Marin, Kentfield, California. In addition, he serves as Project Director for the DeWitt Research Center for Academic Development, San Rafael, California. He has just completed coauthoring the *Screening Test for Auditory Perception (STAP)* (San Rafael, California: Academic Therapy Publications, 1969).

ACADEMIC THERAPY PUBLICATIONS is devoted to the publication of timely and instructive materials for use by parents, teachers, therapists, and other specialists interested in the field of learning disabilities. These materials are made available to facilitate improvement of specialized techniques and to promote a keener awareness and understanding of the problems of children and young adults with basically normal intelligence who manifest learning, perceptual, or behavioral disorders.